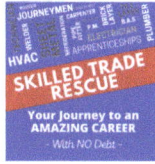

SkilledTradeRescue.com

Building a Balanced Life, The Skilled Trade Worker's Guide
Published by
Legacy Companies, LLC
Hillsboro, OR.

ISBN: 979-8-9873922-1-8
Manufactured in the United States of America

TABLE OF CONTENTS

- o Historical perspective: How did we get here?
- o The unique demands of skilled trades.
- o The consequences of neglecting work-life balance.

- o Antenna UP! Listen to spouses, kids, and friends.
- o Physical, emotional, and mental signs.
- o Extreme impacts of burnout: Alcohol, drug, and food addictions leading to injury and health issues.

- o The power of "No" in professional settings.
- o Evaluating job demands and overtime.
- o Protecting personal and family time.

- o Challenges in this high-tech world.
- o Technology-based Time traps and their impact on work-life balance.
- o Old-school skilled trades are time traps that never go away.
- o BIG MONEY after your eyeballs.
- o Time management concepts that work.

- o The importance of regular exercise.
- o Hobbies and activities outside of work.
- o The role of meditation, mindfulness, and relaxation techniques.

- o Investing in the relationships that matter.
- o The importance of social connections.
- o Building and maintaining a support system.

TABLE OF CONTENTS

Wondering why there is a skilled trade shortage IN THE USA?

D.O.L. Wages

REAL Wages

Department Of Labor reporting skilled trade wages incorrectly for **DECADES.** Mainstream media and politicians ignore it.

Discover More Online

REAL wages are **30% - 60% HIGHER** than D.O.L. reporting fueling labor shortages now reaching critical mass.

THE B.E.S.T. PROCESS?

The B.E.S.T. process offers a holistic approach to personal and professional growth, specifically tailored for skilled trades professionals. While individually significant, each pillar collectively forms a robust framework for achieving a life of success and fulfillment. Let's delve deeper into the essence of each of these pillars:

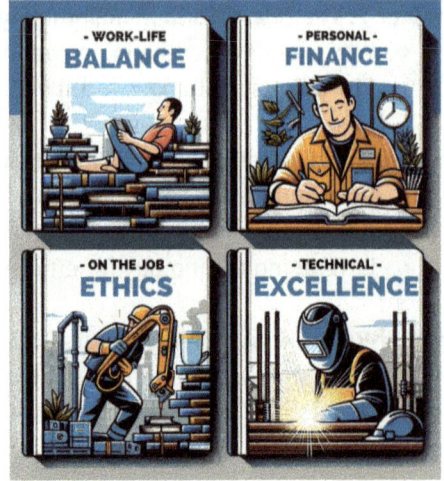

1) Work-Life Balance (B): The first pillar, Work-Life Balance, is the foundation of the B.E.S.T. process. It emphasizes the importance of harmonizing professional responsibilities with personal well-being. In this pillar, you'll explore strategies to effectively manage time, reduce stress, and nurture relationships in and out of the workplace. It's about creating a life where work fuels your passions, and your personal life enriches your professional endeavors. We will cover these concepts in this book.

2) Every Dollar (E): Financial literacy forms the second pillar. Every Dollar is not just about earning but about intelligent earning and spending. This pillar empowers you with the knowledge to make informed financial decisions, establish robust saving habits, and invest wisely. It focuses on building a financial foundation that supports your personal and professional goals, ensuring financial stability and independence. Becoming a millionaire or even a multi-millionaire working in skilled trades is possible. I did it, and so can you.

3) Solid Work Ethic (S): The third pillar, Solid Work Ethic, drives personal and professional achievement. This part of the B.E.S.T. process delves into cultivating a strong, consistent, and ethical approach to work. It's about developing a resilient, dedicated, and continuous improvement mindset. A solid work ethic enhances job performance, personal growth, and satisfaction.

4) Technical Excellence (T): The final pillar, Technical Excellence, is about mastery and proficiency in your chosen trade. This section focuses on acquiring and refining the skills necessary to excel in your field. It includes continuous learning, staying updated with industry trends, and adapting to new technologies and methodologies. Technical excellence increases job satisfaction and opportunities for advancement and complements the other pillars by contributing to a sense of achievement and financial stability.

About This Book

While working on the concepts for a book series designed to help trade professionals avoid my mistakes; I had yet to consider work-life balance initially. Maybe it's the old school in me initially thinking that the pain and suffering that comes with a work-life imbalance is just part of the deal. Then I did some self-reflection and realized that, **YES**, I did struggle with work-life balance, which got my butt in marriage counseling more than once. Here are a few teasers on what we will be getting into in this book:

Boomers had it easier: "Boomer," short for "Baby Boomers," refers to those kids born between 1946 and 1964. The "boom" part happened with military-age men returning from WWII. *These guys got busy making babies.* Back then, work-life balance was challenging at times yet definitely doable. When these folks entered the American workforce, they carried on with pre-WWII work habits. These habits were, for the most part, where conducive to maintaining a work-life balance. For much of their lives, families could survive on only one income. As the years rolled on, these folks got a front-row seat to the digital revolution that was to come. They could see the lights of the ALWAYS ON WORKPLACE train speeding down the tracks toward them.

College obsession: Along with the digital revolution came new narratives that transformed skilled trades from a great way to make a living to what you do when everything else failed. **Result ONE**, over 60% of our youth go to college, creating ever-deepening shortages in skilled trades. **Result TWO,** college students rarely graduate in four years. Even worse, the college curriculum has become a hodgepodge of obscure specializations with limited market value. Result THREE: college debt in America is quickly approaching **TWO TRILLION DOLLARS** with no end in sight.

Skilled Trade Shortages are real: According to the Washington Post, the ratio of skilled trade workers retiring vs. new workers entering the skilled trade workforce is 5:2. From what I can tell, the ratio has never been higher in America, so there is no wonder why work-life imbalance has taken off.

In the following pages, I will share some perspectives, stories, and actionable concepts that skilled trade workers and business owners can try and apply to identify work-life balance imbalances BEFORE they get out of hand. I hope to stave off the bad stuff like deteriorating relationships, parenting challenges, mental health problems, and even personal injuries that have known connections to work-life imbalance.

On a personal note, given a do-over, I'd snatch back some work hours and spend them with my amazing wife, three sons, and a crew of family and friends. That's the heart and soul behind this book, **so let's dive in!**

Introduction

If you work in skilled trades, you may feel the drum beat to work more hours getting louder. **O.T. is a GOOD THING, RIGHT?**

As you read on, I want you to consider the adage that too much of a good thing has consequences. I'm sharing below the **TWO BIG QUESTIONS**. These may be questions you have asked yourself now or are likely to ask yourself in the coming years.

Big Question #1: Why are challenges with work-life balance in skilled trades intensifying?

The COVID-19 pandemic 2020 highlighted long-standing challenges in America's skilled trade labor sector. For decades, there has been a noticeable decline in new entrants into skilled trades relative to population growth. Surprisingly, according to the U.S. Department of Labor, 66% of high school graduates chose college over trade skills before the pandemic. This figure has since decreased a bit to 62% post-pandemic. Simple arithmetic suggests that, considering U.S. population growth, about 65% of high school seniors should enter trades for the next decade to offset the two-decade shortfall. Once parity is reached, a 55% trade to 45% college ratio would maintain equilibrium. Alarmingly, about 40% of the skilled trade workforce is expected to retire or leave within ten years, highlighting the situation's urgency. Unfortunately, things will get worse before they get better.

This shortage is partly due to a persistent stigma around skilled trades, reinforced over the past 20 years. Society has emphasized college education as the ultimate goal, often overshadowing trade careers. Consequently, fewer young people are inclined to pursue trades, creating difficulties for employers in finding suitable replacements for the aging workforce.

Another critical metric to consider is the workforce participation rate, which reflects the proportion of non-disabled individuals engaged in or actively seeking work. The current civilian labor force participation rate is around 62%, indicating that 38% of the eligible workforce is unemployed. Notably, over 7 million non-disabled workers are not actively seeking employment between their mid-twenties and mid-fifties.

In simple terms, work-life balance challenges with our current workforce are understandable, right? Attempting to get an ever-increasing amount of work done with a decreasing number of people causes stress, anxiety, health issues, and even money issues that I will address on the next page.

Introduction (Continued)

Big Question #2: Why are work-life balance problems Intensifing in our personal lives?

The paradox of earning more yet facing personal and health issues stems primarily from "time poverty." As individuals earn more, they often work longer hours, significantly reducing the time available for personal life, family interactions, and relaxation. This scenario leads to an imbalance that can strain relationships and reduce overall life satisfaction. Simultaneously, increased income often brings lifestyle inflation, where spending on luxuries and lifestyle enhancements rises in tandem with earnings. Despite a high income, this pattern can create financial stress if expenses begin to outpace earnings.

You may be wondering how this happens. Well, high-paying jobs typically come with increased responsibilities. For skilled tradespeople, this commonly also comes with physically demanding tasks.

Career advancement and financial success often lead to personal relationships being sidelined. This neglect can cause significant issues in marriages and other close relationships, as these require time and emotional investment. Additionally, high earners frequently deprioritize self-care, including regular health check-ups, exercise, and adequate rest.

Increased prosperity and skilled trade career advancement can bring about psychological challenges, including anxiety and stress related to wealth maintenance and growth. This pressure can adversely affect mental health.

Many skilled trade pros look at these challenges and take them all in stride for a while. Fortunately, although stressful at the time when life is getting out of balance, there are warning signs if you care to look. When these warning signs become front and center, many will unfortunately ignore them, which is a mistake.

My hope for this book is not just to present some of the most common warning signs of imbalance, although this would be great progress. No, my ultimate objective is to share with you the steps you can take to bring your life back into balance. If you can, chances are good that you will travel through the entire arch of your career with your physical and mental health intact. And the bonus of holding on to the lifelong relationships that rode the rollercoaster of life with you.

Introduction *(Continued)*

Otto and Carol: The story of Otto and Carol parallels many American couples. Two ambitious people are in love and looking to live the American Dream. The arch of their story will take you through new love, potential tragedy, and redemption. Their story is rooted in the real world.

Meet Otto: School was tough for Otto for as long as he could remember. The other kids seemed to pick up reading quickly, and it took Otto a LOT longer to retain information through reading. As a result, Otto went through most of his school years thinking he was just dumb. Fortunately for Otto, he had grit to work through reading assignments, sometimes reading the same text two or three times before the information would stick in his brain. Once it stuck, he was good to go.

Despite having moderate *Dyslexia, which would not be officially diagnosed for another twenty years, Otto graduated high school as a "C" student. When Otto came to the college vs. trade crossroads, as many high school students do, Otto effortlessly said **TRADES PLEASE!**

Meet Carol: An excellent student, Carol sailed through high school and almost immediately jumped into the workforce, landing a great job at a high-tech company. Carol quickly realized that the high-tech culture rewarded educated workers with better opportunities, so she started taking night courses at the local JC. Carol was making great money and on her way up the corporate ladder.

NEW LOVE: Their worlds collided one Saturday - a day meant to be just another day. Otto walked into the office of the company he worked at for a training class, and there was Carol, helping her grandmother with some typing and filing. It was a scene from a movie: Otto, the tradesman with a heart of gold, and Carol, the corporate star with a brilliant mind, met that day, and the rest was history. **More about these two later.**

*About Dyslexia: Dyslexia, recognized as a widespread neurodevelopmental disorder, impacts approximately 20% of individuals globally. This condition primarily affects reading skills, characterized by difficulties with accurate and fluent word recognition and poor spelling and decoding abilities. Dyslexia is not merely a challenge in literacy; it often involves difficulties in processing language but does not reflect an individual's overall intelligence. There is a long list of famous people who are known to have dyslexia. These include Tom Cruise, Steven Spielberg, Whoopi Goldberg, and Richard Branson.

Work-Life Balance Check-Up

Before diving into Chapter 1, let's take a moment to briefly assess your work-life balance. This preliminary evaluation aims to understand how well you're integrating your personal and professional responsibilities. As we progress through this book, we'll periodically stop for similar assessments, offering guidance and solutions to manage any work-life imbalances before they become problematic.

Instructions

To enhance your experience and ensure the most accurate results from the work-life balance checkup, consider these recommendations:

Prepare your environment: You can find a calm and comfortable spot where you will most likely be disturbed. This could be a quiet room or a peaceful outdoor setting. Minimize potential distractions. Turn off notifications on your phone and computer, and inform others around you not to disturb you during this time. Ensure good lighting and comfortable seating to maintain focus and avoid physical discomfort.

Timing Checkup: Conduct this checkup when your mind is clear and relaxed, typically within two hours. Avoid taking this checkup during or immediately after work hours, as your current stress or fatigue levels may influence your responses. Consider doing light exercises or meditation before the checkup to clear your mind and reduce stress.

Answering Questions: Understand that this checkup is a tool for self-reflection, and there are no right or wrong answers. Be honest with yourself. The accuracy of this self-evaluation depends on your willingness to be introspective and truthful in your responses.

Approach to Questions: Trust your gut reaction. Your first response is often the most reflective of your true feelings and experiences. Try to spend only a little bit of time on one question. It might be a sign to move on and not overanalyze if you are stuck.

Before Starting: Read through the instructions at the beginning, especially the scoring details. Understanding how your answers will be interpreted can help you approach the questions more effectively. Please take a few deep breaths and clear your mind of other worries. This can help you focus solely on the questions and your responses.

Work-Life Balance Check-Up

Step 1: Read each scenario in the left column. Then, circle a 1, 2, or 3 if..............

1 = RARELY happens | 2 = Happens ONCE IN A WHILE | 3 = Happens ALL THE TIME.

Step 2: Once you have scored each item, write your "Your total Score: >" at the bottom of the page in the box provided.

1) How often do you work beyond your scheduled hours?	1 2 3
2) How often does work get in the way of doing hobbies or personal activities weekly?	1 2 3
3) You think about work during your off hours?	1 2 3
4) You find it challenging to detach from work during vacations or days off.	1 2 3
5) You wake up in the morning NOT feeling well-rested.	1 2 3
6) Your work schedule interfere with family or personal time.	1 2 3
7) Working gets in the way of relaxation and self-care weekly.	1 2 3
8) You miss out on important family or personal events because you are working or feeling burnt out.	1 2 3
9) You come home wanting to relax and end up having an argument with your spouse or kids.	1 2 3
10) You have arguments with your spouse about money.	1 2 3
11) Work responsibilities hinder your physical health or exercise routine.	1 2 3
12) Your work and/or personal life feel out of control.	1 2 3
Your Total Score -- >>	

Work-Life Balance Check-Up

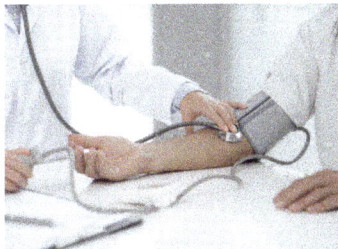

Now that you have finished your checkup, let's look at your total evaluation score and see what this means. Assuming you answered each question with a **1, 2, or 3**, "Your Total Score" will range between **12** and **36**. As you may have concluded, a lower total score would indicate that you have made better progress in work-life balance.

GREAT Work-Life Balance (Score Range: 12-20): Scores in this range generally exhibit a healthy equilibrium between work and personal life. You are adept at keeping work obligations confined to regular business hours and seldom allow responsibilities to come to your time. You usually feel refreshed and have ample opportunity to engage in hobbies and relaxation. You can effectively disconnect from work during vacations and days off and rarely miss family or personal events due to work commitments. **While work-life balance appears to be well-managed, please keep in mind to maintain this harmony.**

AVERAGE Work-Life Balance (Score Range: 21-29): Scoring within this bracket often experiences a moderate challenge in balancing professional and private life. While work occasionally spills over into your time off, it is not a consistent issue. You might occasionally work beyond regular hours or bring work-related thoughts into your off-hours. Sometimes, you need help to carve out time for personal activities or self-care and occasionally have to cancel or reschedule personal commitments due to work demands. **If you live in this category, you should monitor your work-life balance and explore strategies to prevent work from increasingly encroaching on your time.**

POOR Work-Life Balance (Score Range: 30-36): Scoring within this bracket suggests you need help to balance work and personal life. Your work responsibilities often overshadow your time, leading to heightened stress and potential burnout. You tend to work long hours, need help to disconnect from work, and frequently miss out on personal and family activities. You are likely to experience sleep disturbances and high-stress levels due to work-related issues and have minimal time for hobbies, relaxation, and self-care. This score suggests that you need to reevaluate your work habits and priorities. Establishing clear boundaries between work and personal life, seeking support, and prioritizing self-care are essential to achieving a healthier work-life balance.

Regardless of your checkup score, get ready to gain new insights to help you build on current strengths and address potential weaknesses holding you back from **lasting work-life balance.**

Chapter 1
Understanding the Work-Life Imbalance

In This Chapter

- Exploring America's evolving work attitudes over the years.

- The nostalgic era of balanced work-life in the post-war economy.

- Consumerism's rise leads to longer working hours.

- Digital age's impact on work-life boundaries.

- Skilled trades' changing dynamics in the American consciousness.

Chapter 1 of the book examines the evolution of work attitudes in America, particularly in skilled trades, and the impact on work-life balance. It nostalgically recalls the balanced post-WWII era, then details the rise of consumerism and the digital age, leading to longer work hours and blurred work-life boundaries. The chapter highlights the diminished value of skilled trades in favor of white-collar jobs, exacerbated by labor shortages and technological advancements.

It concludes by discussing this imbalance's physical and mental tolls and the unique pressures facing skilled trade workers today.

"The key is not to prioritize what's on your schedule, but to schedule your priorities."

Stephen Covey, the author of "The 7 Habits of Highly Effective People."

Learn more online about this chapter

Chapter 1
Understanding the Work-Life Imbalance
-Historical perspective: How did we get here?-

Let's start this chapter with a quick trip back up the road of history to get some perspectives on how the attitude of work has changed over the years in America. Yes, I understand that history can be a bit boring; however, understanding what America's working class was like in the past may help with two important things.

First, America's evolution gives us some amazing things from which we (and the World) have benefitted greatly. I won't bore you with the list; let's say that if you are an American citizen, you have already won the lottery of life.

Second, and probably even more significant, the advancements we all enjoy have come at a cost, and work-life balance is one of the more modern casualties of America's success. Good news! With some learning, persistence, and sincere effort, you CAN get your life back while still enjoying the American Dream. The American Dream is still possible; it is a bit harder to find nowadays.

The Golden Age of Balance: Back in the day, Gramps had a 9-to-5 job punctuated by coffee breaks, solid lunch hours, and clocking out at a specific HARD STOP time. It might sound like something from a nostalgic movie, but there was a time when Work-life balance wasn't just a catchphrase but a way of life. The economy was booming in the post-WWII era, especially in the 50s and 60s. Jobs were abundant, wages were decent, and most families could survive and thrive on a single income. Dad could work at the local factory, and Mom, if she chose to, could stay home, raise the kids, and manage the household. The weekends? They were for rest, relaxation, and a bit of fun. Bored yet?

The Rise of Consumerism: Things started to change as the years passed. The 70s and 80s saw a massive shift. Hello, credit cards, and goodbye, savings! We wanted bigger houses, flashier cars, and the latest gadgets. In came the day if you don't have this or that, you are just not cool or perhaps even a loser. Marketing brains (Mad Men) worked

tirelessly to figure out how to separate us from the hard-earned dollar. Well, at least that has not changed. We needed more money to get all this STUFF, which meant more work hours or multiple jobs. The demands of the job began to creep into personal time. No longer was it just about putting food on the table; it was about LIVING LARGE and ensuring everyone could see it. The term "keeping up with the Joneses" became a cliche.

Chapter 1
Understanding the Work-Life Imbalance
-Historical perspective: How did we get here?-

Tech Boom and The "Always-On" Culture: Enter the 90s and the 2000s: the dawn of the digital age. With the rise of the internet, smartphones, and laptops, work began to follow us everywhere. Remember the first time you got that work email on your phone during dinner? Probably not; that was tens of thousands of emails ago; come on, man!

They're calling on the cell, so they must REALLY NEED ME. Makes you feel important, right? Soon, those emails started pouring in all the time. Suddenly, the boundaries between "work" and "life" began to blur a bit. Still boring? For skilled trade workers, especially business owners, this meant being available round the clock for customer calls, last-minute fixes, and emergencies. So much for the hard stop, and it's time to go home now. What the heck is that?

To see how fast things were changing during this time, check out HBO's miniseries "Silicon Valley." This series highlights the digital revolution and the meteoric rise of tech giants like Facebook, Google, and Amazon. Venture capital fueled a fiercely competitive start-up culture, leading to innovative disruptions in various industries by companies like Uber and Airbnb. This period also saw a cultural shift in workplace norms and the profound impact of social media on communication and society. However, it was accompanied by challenges such as data privacy concerns and the ethical implications of advanced technologies, making this era a blend of remarkable growth and significant cautionary lessons.

Skilled Trades in a Changing World: For our skilled trade community, there was another layer to this evolving situation. The respect and value for hands-on trades began to wane in the face of glamorous tech jobs and office gigs. Many started to believe that success was only defined by white-collar jobs.

Big-name brand companies started to firewall off high-paying jobs, particularly in technology, for folks with college degrees. For the first time in America, the swag of working with your hands started losing appeal. What got lost in America's consciousness while the dirty jobs took the back seat to clean, cushy office gigs was that most amazing technology depended highly on skilled trades. The average Gen Z could not comprehend without skilled trades, major technologies like YouTube, Google, and TikTok would not exist. What's worse is that civil society as we know it would fall apart if skilled tradespeople were not around to keep critical infrastructure working.

Chapter 1
Understanding the Work-Life Imbalance
-Historical perspective: How did we get here?-

The "you must go to college" narrative broke out, mainly powered by the ever-growing college machine (and its lobby), with an increasingly corrupt mainstream media more than willing to promote it.

Sprinkle in our government, lending an endless supply of cash to our college kids, and you end up with over 62% of our kids going to college and soon to be strapped to **TWO TRILLION dollars in college debt that is not backruptable.**

Our political leaders and media ignore changing data about the college vs. trades question. A case in point is the graphic below, which shows tending that began in 2018 and accelerated after the 2020 pandemic. Non-college degree wages jumped past those with a college degree. Since skilled trades wages tend to be higher per capita, this graphic indicates a real supply and demand problem likely in skilled trade professions. This is good news from a wages standpoint but could be better for work-life balance in the trades.

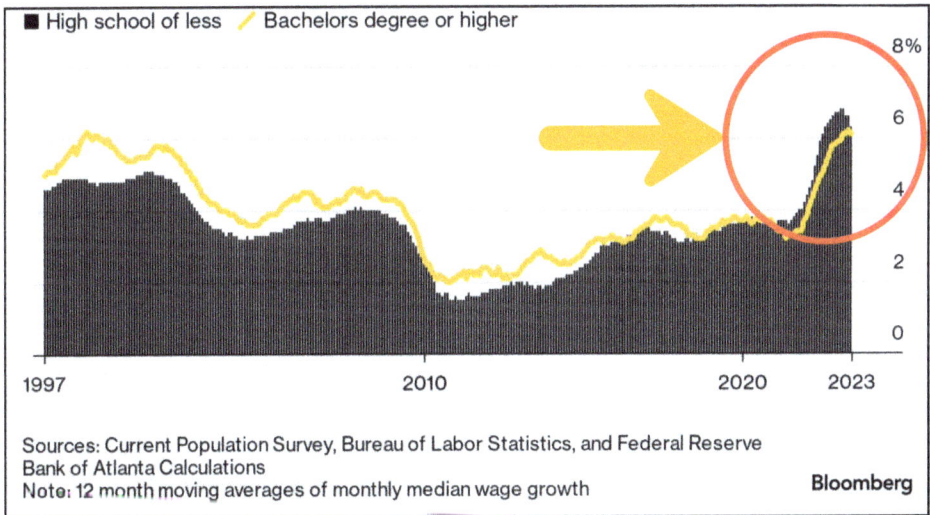

Sources: Current Population Survey, Bureau of Labor Statistics, and Federal Reserve Bank of Atlanta Calculations
Note: 12 month moving averages of monthly median wage growth

Bloomberg

The Present Scenario: Today, fueled by the labor shortage, the idea of a work-life balance seems like a luxury for many. As America's skilled labor shortages continue to intensify, workers are being asked to fill the gap, creating feelings like there's no off switch. This situation presents a multifaceted challenge. Not only is there the physical toll of the job but also the mental stress of managing a business, keeping up with technological advancements, and ensuring customer satisfaction in an "instant gratification" society.

Chapter 1
Understanding the Work-Life Imbalance
-The unique demands of skilled trades-

On the surface, the following points may represent a challenge, AKA turn-off, and I get that. Like most things in life, some of the best opportunities we will ever have are initially rooted in challenges, **so stick with me.**

Sense of urgency like never before: Whom do they call when someone's sink springs a leak, or the lights start flickering? That's right – they call us. Skilled trades have been the backbone of our society for centuries. And while white-collar folks might be dealing with spreadsheets and PowerPoint slides, tradespeople work with their hands, getting dirty. When demand gets ahead of supply in any marketplace, the result is an elevated sense of urgency.

For example, during the 2020 pandemic, toilet paper was perceived to be in short supply. As a result, urgency set in, and folks got a little testy with retailers who needed to limit how much they could buy. Although the skilled trade shortage is less dramatic than a pandemic (at least not yet), trade businesses are feeling the pain of too much work (demand) and their ability to get all of the work done (supply). This has created a sense of urgency that is building slowly. At some point, America will wake up to some of the stressful realities that are indeed inbound on all of us, and it won't be pretty.

9-to-5, what's that?: Due to supply/demand urgency, skilled trades no longer fit neatly into that mythical 9-to-5 workday of yesteryear. As with the toilet paper example, customers are getting increasingly testy when they hear, "Sorry, I don't have anyone available," as they are standing in a building with NO POWER. Our current workforce is putting in the hours even when faced with staggering demand, at least for now. Demand will eventually reach critical mass, meaning real emergencies will pop up. At that point, America will wake up to the shortage of skilled trades.

Is there a story here for the mainstream media? I would say yes. They don't care. As mentioned, they will start to care when YouTube, FaceBook, or TikTok go offline due to low facility skilled trade staffing shortages.

Physical Toll = Increase cost of goods and services: Skilled trades demand more than expertise and knowledge; they ask for physical stamina. Tradespeople (who, at least for now, are still humans) are being asked to work more hours and will face higher work-related injuries.

Chapter 1
Understanding the Work-Life Imbalance
-The unique demands of skilled trades-

The costs of caring for these folks will be added to the prices of most products and services. Extended wait times to repair or fix things will add to the fun.

Riding the Waves of Demand: Some trades are also seasonal. Roofers might be swamped during the drier months but find business slowing down when the rain starts. HVAC technicians might run off their feet during summer and winter peaks but find a lull in between. This inconsistency is more than just a logistical headache; it means the pressure is on to make the most of the busy times, often leading to longer hours and fewer breaks.

A Tribe Apart, some good news: Despite these challenges, there's a camaraderie in the trades that's hard to find elsewhere. The shared experiences, the mutual respect for a job well done, and the genuine satisfaction of fixing, building, and creating. But it's also essential to recognize the unique pressures that come with the territory. You would think this would be a compelling story, yet close-up looks at skilled trades remain ignored by the mainstream media for the most part.

GOOD NEWS!

Skilled Trade Workers post higher job satisfaction than many occupations requiring four-year degrees.

GOOD NEWS!

Blue vs White Collar Job Satisfaction Data

Skilled labor career satisfaction remains steady at 83%. Depending on the study you look at, skilled trade's overall job satisfaction trends are 15% higher than white-collar careers that require a four-year bachelor degree.

Job Satisfaction
IN THE SKILLED TRADES

83% **Career Satisfaction**

20% Global Employee Engagement

34% US Employee Engagement

Chapter 1
Understanding the Work-Life Imbalance
-The consequences of neglecting work-life balance -

And finally, for this chapter, we will look at some of the real consequences when skilled trade professionals neglect work-life balance.

Many of you may know this drill., a quick dinner, maybe a bit of telly, and it's off to bed. **Rinse and repeat.** For many in the skilled trades, this isn't just a once-in-a-while kind of day; it's the norm. But what happens when we're so wrapped up in the grind that our time and health get left in the dust? Let's dive into that:

Health Ain't Just Physical: First and foremost, when discussing health, it isn't just the bumps, bruises, and backaches. Yeah, those are part of the deal, especially in a physically demanding gig, as touched on already. But we're also talking about the noggin – your mental well-being. Skipping breaks, working long hours, and neglecting personal time can lead to stress, anxiety, and even depression. And trust me, when the mind isn't right, everything else starts to crumble, too.

Relationships on the Rocks: Have you ever snapped at a loved one after a long day? When work dominates our time and energy, relationships can suffer. It's not just about missing events; it's the daily disconnect, the lack of quality time, and the emotional exhaustion that makes it hard to be present even when you're physically there. Later in this book, I will cover some warning signs you may be missing; I know I did.

Burnout's a Real Thing: You've probably heard of burnout. It isn't just some fancy term that folks in offices use. Burnout is real, and it hits hard. It's that feeling of total exhaustion where you're mentally, emotionally, and physically drained. It's when the job you once loved starts to feel like a ball and chain. And for those in the skilled trades, burnout can be especially dangerous because a foggy mind can lead to mistakes, accidents, and injuries. Is nodding off at the wheel, not out of the ordinary? Wait until you hear about what happened to Otto later in this book.

Missing Out on Life's Moments: Life's made up of moments – big and small. Your daughter's first steps, a spontaneous road trip, or even a lazy Sunday afternoon nap. Missed your kid's soccer game because a job ran late. When work becomes all-consuming, these moments can slip right by. And once they're gone, well, you can't get them back.

Chapter 1
Understanding the Work-Life Imbalance
-The consequences of neglecting work-life balance -

Financial Strains: Now, this one seems counterintuitive. More work means more money, right? Well, only sometimes. Those paychecks will get fat if you are a trades pro or a business owner and that's rewarding.

Finally, you see the fruits of your labors, and it feels good as it should. Can you feel that? I know I did.

Here is something that I experienced personally, and a high percentage of the trade pros I talked to on the podcast have also run into. With more money, a false sense of financial security can creep in. This commonly leads to spending outpacing income.

Funny thing about money. As spending decisions become more emotional, the brain starts messing with you. When faced with a buying decision, the quick draw on the credit cards connects to thoughts like, I work hard, I deserve this, I will pay it off next month etc...

The giveaway that spending is getting out of control is when you look honestly at your home, shop, and yard and see stuff you are not using as much (or at all) as you thought you would when you purchased it. How many pairs of golf shoes, fishing poles, or hunting rifles do you NEED around anyway?

What makes matters more challenging on the spending front is when your work life starts getting out of whack. You are tired, stressed, etc, and your financial decision-making tends to move into the reality distortion bubble. When this happens, the money you spend outside of what you need to live becomes predominantly based on emotions. So, the vicious cycle of working even harder to service spending habits and the associated debt ratchets into high gear.

There is a silver lining to this. Of all the challenges skilled trade professionals experience during their careers, money challenges are the most solvable if given effort, dedication, and time.

The dreaded "B" = Budget! I will discuss money in more detail later in this book. When we get to that, I will provide some strategies to help with money problems when they appear. These strategies will NOT be sexy, yet they DO work.

"A budget is telling your money where to go instead of wondering where it went." **- Dave Ramsey - Author of "The Total Money Makeover", national Finance Guru.**

Chapter 1
Understanding the Work-Life Imbalance
-The consequences of neglecting work-life balance -

Otto and Carol - Troubles in the Wind: Fast forward a bit, and we find Otto and Carol married and thriving. Otto's the guy everyone loved to work for - the human equivalent of a morning coffee, bringing energy and positivity. Carol? She's killing it. Her work ethic is a force to be reckoned with.

Otto, like his father (who grew up during the great depression), had an inherent drive to get ahead no matter what it took, and, at least at first, it resulted in lucrative opportunities for the family business.

Both working hard and making great money, they purchased their first home, symbolizing their hard work and love. But as Otto's business grows, so do the demands on his time. Carol's once-small worries about how hard Otto worked begin to take root. After log days, Otto finds solace in having a beer or two or FIVE. Over time, Otto's drinking habit slowly started casting a shadow over their dream.

As Otto became increasingly engrossed in his work, Carol began feeling distant from Otto. So much so that Carol stated she was seeing a marriage counselor on her own to try and sort out her feelings. She tried several times to have Otto join her; however, he was just too busy repeatedly reclining. Carol eventually got enough tools from counseling to keep the lines of communication open with Otto; however, the challenges were far from resolved.

A year later, despite their early marital challenges, Otto and Carol were blessed with twin sons. The family construction business was booming, allowing Carol to become a full-time Mom. The boys were growing so fast. These two were living the dream, and Little did either of these newlyweds know that there was some real trouble brewing.

For a while, the work-life imbalance that had started to pop early in their marriage was replaced with the intense activity of having two new babies. Initially, Otto and Carol felt they had settled into how things would be. These two were used to working hard, so they dug in and got it done. Wake up, take care of the kids, work, have dinner, watch a little TV, and go back to bed. As the cliche goes, rinse and repeat.

What these two did not realize was that their early marital challenges were still there and would eventually create even more intense challenges.

Chapter 2
Symptoms of Imbalance Working in Skilled Trades

In This Chapter

- Antenna up! Spotting work-life imbalance through family feedback.

- Children's behavior as a balance indicator.

- Friends' observations reveal work's dominance.

- Physical symptoms signal excessive work.

- Emotional changes due to imbalance.

- Mental fog and decision-making issues.

- Relationship strains from work stress.

- Burnout: More than just fatigue.

- Workplace stress leads to injury.

Chapter 2 of the book explores the signs of work-life imbalance in skilled trades. It emphasizes the importance of being attentive to feedback from family and friends, who can often spot early signs of imbalance. The chapter delves into various indicators, such as physical symptoms, emotional changes, and mental fog, emphasizing how these factors can negatively impact relationships and overall well-being. It also highlights the extreme impacts of burnout, including substance abuse and health issues, illustrating how neglecting work-life balance can have serious consequences.

"Choose a job you love, and you will never have to work a day in your life."

– Confucius - Chinese philosopher and educator

Learn more online about this chapter

Chapter 2
Symptoms of Imbalance Working in Skilled Trades
Antenna UP! Listen to spouse, kids, and friends.

Work-life imbalance can creep into our lives so subtly that it often goes unnoticed until it takes a toll on our health, relationships, and overall well-being. Particularly in the skilled trades, where the job demands can be physically and mentally taxing, maintaining a balance can sometimes feel like an elusive goal. How do you know if your life is out of whack? Sometimes, the most telling signs come not from our feelings but from those closest to us. Our spouses, children, and friends can offer valuable insights into how we're faring, provided that we pay attention.

Feedback from the Home Front: It's not unusual for a tradesperson to come home after a long day feeling drained and wanting nothing but to relax. But if your significant other remarks about your constant exhaustion or lack of physical or mental presence, it's important to take a moment and reflect <u>BEFORE</u> lashing out, as many, especially men, do.

Early warnings: Have you ever noticed a recurring theme in the feedback you get from loved ones like your significant other? Phrases like, "You're always so tired," "You never have time for us," "Even when you are physically here, your mind is always somewhere else," or "Work is all you ever talk about," could be subtle warning signs that your work is overtaking other facets of your life. Later in this book, we will delve into the "emotional bank account" concept that will shed more light on warning signs.

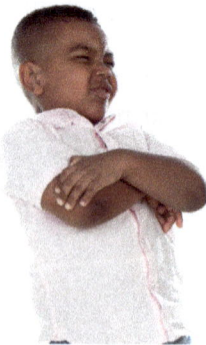

Kids Know Best: If your kids often lament about you missing their school events or not having time for play, it might be more than just typical childhood complaints. They might be picking up on a deeper issue. Their feelings, although expressed in simpler terms, can be a barometer for the overall health of your work-life dynamic. Depending on the age and personality of your kids, they may need help to verbalize how your skilled trade occupation impacts them. In many cases, kids will act out, displaying disruptive or antisocial behaviors that could be a warning sign.

The impact of parental life balance on children's well-being is complex and multifaceted. A research paper from Child Development Perspectives touches on a key aspect of this topic, emphasizing that children who perceive an imbalance in their parents' lives can suffer negative consequences such as increased stress, anxiety, and academic difficulties. Yes, feedback from our kids can be one of the most honest indicators of adult imbalance in this household.

Chapter 2
Symptoms of Imbalance Working in Skilled Trades
Antenna UP! Listen to spouse, kids, and friends.

Real Friends vs. Acquaintances: Unlike immediate family, your earliest warning signs will tend to come from your friends. An interesting conundrum of our always-connected times is that the lines between our friends and acquaintances have blurred. Let's explore the subject of true friendships and acquaintances for a moment. This could help you avoid getting advice from people with little to no vested interest in your well-being, which can be dangerous.

Applications like FaceBook and Instagram make it possible to expand our world with just a few clicks. This amazing connectivity has separated humans from one of our basic needs. This would be in person-to-person, face-to-face interactions. As a result, the concept of what a "Friend" is has become nuanced, which is an understatement. For the first time in history, friendship has evolved to include people we rarely, or in some cases never, interact with in person.

The graphic below is a play on a puzzle concept (Where's Waldo) developed in 1986 by Martin Handford. There are three types of relationships in this illustration. First, the workers standing around at ground level. These folks are Waldo's acquaintances. Next are a few workers, also at the ground level, who are raising their hands. These folks are strong acquaintances, perhaps coworkers; however, they are not real friends. Lastly, the folks standing up are Waldo's real friends. Considering our always-connected world, Waldo's entire crowd in this image would have been about one-third of this size just a decade ago.

On the next page, we will look into some measurable things to look for in real friends. This is nothing new here, yet it's talked about these days.

Chapter 2
Symptoms of Imbalance Working in Skilled Trades
Antenna UP! Listen to spouse, kids, and friends.

Real Friends vs Acquaintances: Real friends and acquaintances represent two distinct types of relationships we encounter in our social lives, each playing a unique role with different levels of emotional investment and intimacy.

Depth and Intimacy: Real friends are characterized by deeper intimacy and understanding. We share personal experiences, thoughts, and feelings with them. This deeper connection often stems from shared experiences, mutual interests, or an emotional bond nurtured over time. In contrast, acquaintances are people we know but with whom we have a superficial relationship. We might interact with these folks individuals regularly, such as coworkers or neighbors, but our conversations and interactions tend to be more about general topics and less about personal issues.

Emotional Support and Trust: One of the key aspects of friendship is providing emotional support. Friends are the people we turn to in times of need, who offer a shoulder to lean on during tough times and celebrate with us during happy occasions. This relationship is built on a foundation of trust and mutual respect. Acquaintances, while they might offer support in a more general sense, typically do not play a significant role in providing emotional support. The level of trust we share with acquaintances is also more limited than our deep trust in real friends.

Frequency and Nature of Interaction: Real friends are typically individuals we interact with more frequently and in various settings. These interactions are routine and often sought out for mutual enjoyment and companionship. With acquaintances, interactions are often limited to specific settings or occasions and tend to be less frequent and more structured. For instance, you might chat with an acquaintance at a weekly meeting or greet a neighbor when you see them, but these interactions don't generally extend beyond their specific contexts.

Role in Personal Growth and Development: Real friends often play a significant role in our personal growth and development. They influence our perspectives, help us through personal challenges, and contribute to our sense of identity. The deep conversations and experiences shared with friends can shape our beliefs and values. While acquaintances can offer different viewpoints and be a part of our social network, they typically play a limited role in our personal development.

Chapter 2
Symptoms of Imbalance Working in Skilled Trades
Antenna UP! Listen to spouse, kids, and friends.

Expectations and Obligations: Real friends' expectations and obligations are generally greater than in relationships with acquaintances. Real friends often expect a higher level of commitment from each other regarding time, emotional support, and loyalty. These expectations are usually mutual and are part of what strengthens the bond of friendship. In contrast, the expectations from acquaintances are minimal, primarily revolving around basic social courtesy and respect.

While real friends and acquaintances are important in our social lives, they serve distinctly different purposes. A deeper emotional connection, mutual support, and a significant role in personal development characterize real friendships. In contrast, acquaintances are characterized by a more superficial connection and limited emotional involvement, often confined to specific contexts or casual interactions.

Now, let's look at some early warning signs of work-life imbalances commonly appearing with real friends before challenges start at home.

Real Friends as Mirrors: Our real friends, especially those outside of our professional circles, offer an external perspective that can be incredibly enlightening. It's common for real friends to make observations about our lifestyles that we have yet to notice ourselves. They might point out how infrequently meeting, highlighting the need for more interactions outside of a professional setting. This can be a subtle indicator of how engrossed we have become in our work lives, potentially at the expense of personal relationships and social engagements.

Another indicator is that real friends often notice patterns in our conversations. They might observe that our discussions predominantly revolve around work-related topics. This consistent focus on professional matters during casual conversations can indicate that our work identity overshadows our identity. It's a reminder of the importance of nurturing and maintaining a balance between our professional and personal lives.

The insights and comments of real friends are invaluable. They provide a mirror through which we can see the imbalances in our lives, offering us a chance to recalibrate and enrich our personal experiences. Such observations encourage us to consider stepping back, reflecting, and making necessary adjustments in our lifestyle to ensure a more well-rounded and fulfilling life.

Chapter 2
Symptoms of Imbalance Working in Skilled Trades
Antenna UP! Listen to spouse, kids, and friends.

Here is some interesting data supporting the trend away from real friendships that have only accelerated since this study was conducted in 2015.

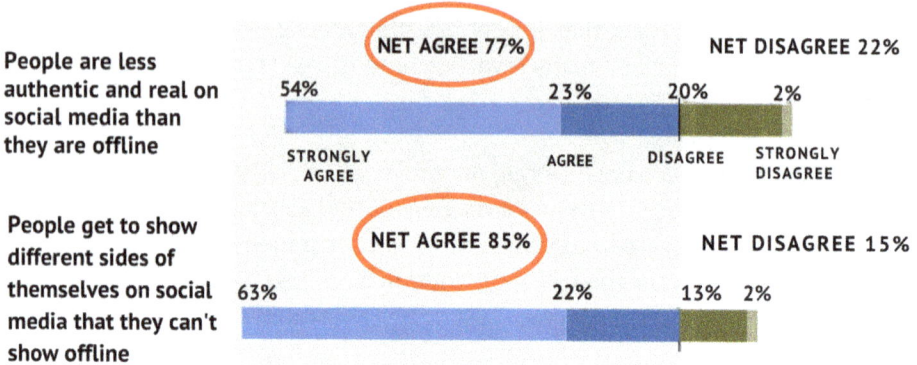

People are less authentic and real on social media than they are offline

NET AGREE 77%   NET DISAGREE 22%

54%   23%   20%   2%

STRONGLY AGREE   AGREE   DISAGREE   STRONGLY DISAGREE

People get to show different sides of themselves on social media that they can't show offline

NET AGREE 85%   NET DISAGREE 15%

63%   22%   13%   2%

Source: Pew Research Center's Teen Relationship Survey. Sept. 25-Oct. 9, 2014, and Feb. 10-March 16, 2015. Due to rounding, net values many not add up to 100%

The graphic above highlights Gen Z's challenges in this modern digital age. Gen Z individuals relying heavily on digital communication may find developing and maintaining friendships in real life challenging.

Face-to-face interactions involve nuances such as body language, tone of voice, and immediate feedback, which are absent in digital communication. Consequently, overreliance on social media can lead to a lack of development in these critical social skills.

Furthermore, social media interactions can be superficial, lacking the depth and authenticity typically found in real-life friendships. The emphasis on curated personas and the pressure to present a perfect image can lead to decreased self-esteem and increased social comparison, which are detrimental to mental well-being.

Something to consider: Interpersonal connections initiated through social media, especially those with limited to no in-person interactions, rarely evolve into real friendships, as defined in this chapter.

Chapter 2
Symptoms of Imbalance Working in Skilled Trades
Physical Signs: When Your Body Rings the Alarm

So you have received the early warning signs from family and friends. Now, let's look at some additional personal inventory that is NOT a matter of opinion. Your body will NEVER lie to you, so let's look at some physical signs that are expected when your work-life balance gets out of whack.

It's amazing how attuned our bodies are to the overall balance (or imbalance) of our lives. Physical health often takes early hits when things are skewed towards excessive work. The signs are even more pronounced in skilled trades, where the job can be quite demanding compared to an office gig.

For starters, **chronic fatigue** is a common work-life imbalance red flag. We're not just talking about the usual end-of-day tiredness; this is waking up exhausted even after a full night's sleep. According to a study by the National Sleep Foundation, those who reported poor work-life balance were nearly twice as likely to sleep poorly, opening the door for chronic fatigue.

Constant stress can also wreak havoc on your immune system. When your cortisol levels (the stress hormone) are consistently high, they suppress your immune function, making you more prone to catching colds and flu.

A 2020 survey by Gallup found that among employees who strongly agree they often feel burned out at work, 63% are more likely to take a sick day, and 23% are more likely to visit the emergency room. The physical toll of burnout isn't just in your head—it's real, and it affects both your work and personal life.

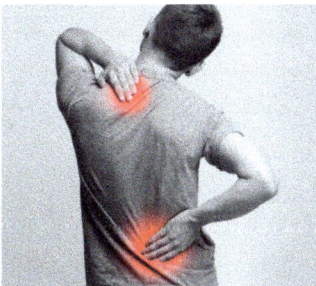

Musculoskeletal problems - The strain on the body from these trades often leads to more than just temporary discomfort; it can evolve into long-term degenerative conditions. For instance, consistent heavy lifting or awkward postures can accelerate joint wear and tear, leading to osteoarthritis, particularly in the knees and hips. Similarly, repetitive tasks can result in overuse injuries such as tendonitis or bursitis, which can become chronic if not properly addressed; moreover, inadequate recovery time and poor workplace ergonomics can exacerbate these issues, increasing the risk of serious injuries like herniated discs or rotator cuff tears. Therefore, skilled trade workers must adopt preventive strategies, such as using proper lifting techniques, taking regular breaks to stretch and move, and using assistive devices to reduce strain. Early intervention and appropriate medical care are key to managing these conditions effectively and preventing long-term disability.

Symptoms of Imbalance Working in Skilled Trades

Physical Signs: When Your Body Rings the Alarm

Small annoyances you'd usually brush off suddenly feel like the last straw, causing you to lash out. Unfortunately, family and friends are the first to get the brunt of such lashouts. According to a report by the American Psychological Association, almost half of all adults report snapping or getting angry easily when stressed. Oh, shocker, right? :-)

Feelings of detachment: From loved ones is another warning sign of imbalance. You might find that when you have free time, you're less emotionally present than you'd like. The passion and enthusiasm you once had for hobbies or spending time with family and friends will dwindle.

The insidious things about detachment patterns will likely occur over a long period. So slow that your stress-induced reality distortion field may think everything is just hunky dory when in reality, it's NOT. The downside is that family and friends will see it first, as covered earlier. Unfortunately, they often avoid bringing things up until they reach a point of lashing out themselves, creating situations where things are said on both sides that you can't take back.

Lastly, skilled tradespeople might grapple with feelings of guilt. Whether missing out on your child's soccer game or skipping a friend's birthday party because you're too tired or have work commitments, this continuous tug-of-war between personal life and work can result in a heavy emotional burden that only adds to stress and emotional detachment.

Mental Signs - When The Mind Gets Foggy: Mentally, the effects of work-life imbalance can manifest in several ways. The most evident are reduced concentration and memory lapses. Have you ever walked into a room and forgot why? Or did you start a task and get distracted midway?

Decision-making: Becomes more challenging. Tasks that used to be a breeze suddenly can become seemingly insurmountable mountains. You might even notice a reduction in your problem-solving skills. This specific sign of work-life imbalance can hit home when you are a business owner. Your employees and even customers you work with regularly will likely notice something is off with you rather quickly. Before you know it, employees are leaving because of a lack of confidence, and your business is missing out on opportunities all because you are out of balance.

Chapter 2
Symptoms of Imbalance Working in Skilled Trades

Extreme impacts of burnout

Anxiety and depression due to prolonged stress, and imbalance can lead to anxiety and depression. A survey by the Mental Health Foundation found that two-thirds of people who reported poor work-life balance also experienced negative mental health symptoms related to their job.

To deal with burnout's physical, mental, and emotional challenges, some skilled trade workers can get caught up in downward spiral situations with moderate to severe consequences.

Alcohol and Drug Addictions: One of the most concerning impacts of burnout in the skilled trades is the tendency for individuals to seek relief through unhealthy coping mechanisms, such as alcohol, drugs, and excessive food consumption.

A study published in The Journal of Occupational and Environmental Medicine found a strong correlation between work-related stress and substance use. When we're mentally and physically drained, it becomes all too tempting to turn to substances that offer a quick escape.

- **Alcohol:** A few beers after a long day might seem harmless, but when a few becomes a few too many, regularly, we're heading into dangerous territory. Like many things, some good/fun things can have the opposite effect. Drinking in excess, especially at the end of the day, can lead to dramatic reductions in rem sleep, weight gain, blood sugar instability, and other negative health effects.

- **Drugs:** One of the most common traps skilled trade workers find themselves in is prescription medication addiction following a doctor's treatment for Musculoskeletal problems that are common in trades.

Food, The Subtle Coping Mechanism: While alcohol and drugs often get the spotlight when discussing addiction, there's a quieter but equally detrimental coping mechanism lurking in the shadows: food addiction. Studies show that individuals experiencing higher stress levels are likelier to crave and consume foods high in fat, sugar, and salt, aka comfort foods. Think about it: after an exhaustive day, doesn't the allure of a greasy pizza or a sugary dessert seem almost irresistible? Using food as a coping mechanism is VERY common with skilled trade workers.

Chapter 2
Symptoms of Imbalance Working in Skilled Trades

Otto and Carol - Troubles have arrived. It became increasingly harder for Otto to turn his brain off. His drinking dramatically increased, and fast food became the norm, leading to high blood pressure, digestive issues, and other health problems. Home life was a challenge as well. The boys always argued, and Carol tried to hold marriage and family together.

One of the biggest causes of friction in her marriage was Otto's complete denial of anything wrong. He would go to work early, come home late, eat, have a few beers, work some more, and go to bed late.

It was a Monday morning; like most days, Otto woke up tired, only getting about three hours of sleep, which had become the norm. When he climbed into his truck that morning, he had no idea that his life would change just a few miles away.

Leaving his subdivision at about 6:30 AM, Otto turned onto a two-lane country road like he did every morning. Getting up to speed, about 60 miles per hour, it was clear sailing to his office just a few miles away. Otto had a huge day getting bids out, dealing with needy customers, and ensuring the workers he managed had everything they needed to complete the day's workload.

And then it happened: Otto fell asleep at the wheel, ran off the road, and rolled his truck down a 30-foot embankment. After the truck was well into its fourth full roll, Otto woke up, and all he could do was yell and hold on for dear life. Then things went dark when Otto whacked his head on the steering wheel.

Otto woke up several hours later in a hospital room with Carol. A while later, that doctor and two police officers entered the room. Otto learned that he fell asleep at the wheel and was the only one injured. The officers shared that Otto's brand-new truck was a goner. The doctor shared that Otto had suffered a concussion and some minor lacerations, yet overall, he was going to be okay. Then, the doctor shared some unexpected news. As part of the emergency triage, complete blood panels had been run. The doctor shared with Otto that she rarely saw blood work that bad. The Doc informed Otto that he would not be alive much longer if he did not make changes to improve his health. The Doc explained that all she could do was prescribe more and more drugs to offset the poor health choices Otto was making; however, that was a short-term solution. It was at that moment that Otto reached a turning point.

Chapter 2 - Checkup

As we wrap up Chapter 2, it's time to evaluate the presence and extent of common symptoms of work-life imbalance affecting you. Like before, upon the completion of this checkup questionnaire, you will calculate a total score. Should your results indicate a significant imbalance, an action plan with targeted suggestions for enhancement will be provided to assist in bettering your condition.

Instructions

As in the prior check-up, please consider the following guidelines in preparing to do this assessment:

Set Up Your Space: You can choose a quiet and cozy area where interruptions are unlikely, such as a quiet room or a tranquil place outdoors. Eliminate distractions by turning off notifications on your devices and letting those around you know you shouldn't be bothered now. Ensure the lighting and seating are adequate to keep your focus sharp and prevent discomfort.

Choose the Right Time: Opt for when you feel most alert and at ease, usually within the first two hours after waking. Refrain from evaluating during or right after working hours, as feelings of stress or tiredness could skew your answers. Engaging in mild exercise or meditation beforehand can help declutter your mind and lessen tension.

Responding to Questions: Please be aware of the assessment as a means for personal contemplation without correct or incorrect replies. I think your honesty is crucial. The effectiveness of this self-check relies on your readiness to look inward and answer truthfully.

Question Approach: Go with your initial instinct. Your first thought typically mirrors your genuine sentiments and life situations. Avoid lingering too long on a single query. If hesitating, consider it a cue to proceed and not dwell excessively.

Preparation for the Evaluation: Review the guidelines provided initially, particularly those about scoring. I know how your responses will be evaluated, which can help tackle the questions with insight. Could you take a moment to breathe deeply and push aside any other concerns? This preparation enables you to concentrate entirely on the questions and your answers.

Chapter 2 - Checkup

Step 1: Read each scenario in the left column. Then, circle a 1, 2, or 3 if..............

1 = RARELY happens | 2 = Happens ONCE IN A WHILE | 3 = Happens ALL THE TIME.

Step 2: Once you have scored each item, write your "Your total Score: >" at the bottom of the page in the box provided.

1) There are days that you feel burnt out and just don't feel liking going into work.		1 2 3
2) You feel like having alcohol or recreational drugs are the only way to get your brain out of work mode.		1 2 3
3) You fell back neck or shoulder discomfort.		1 2 3
4) You experience intermittent or constant feelings of detachment.		1 2 3
5) You thinking or reasoning gets foggy.		1 2 3
6) Your kids complain or even lash out about your absence from home.		1 2 3
7) Conversations with your significant others are limited to small talk.		1 2 3
8) Your friends are starting to complain about how much you are working.		1 2 3
9) Friends or family are starting to comment that you talk about work to much.		1 2 3
10) While engaging with social media or video games, time gets away from you.		1 2 3
11) I feel that my job negatively impacts my personal identity and satisfaction.		1 2 3
12) I find myself purchasing things that become boring within a few weeks and then just sitting around.		1 2 3
Your Total Score --	>>	

After you complete your assessment, please look at the interpretation of your calculated score below. Celebrate your achievement if you find yourself with a "LOW" score! You are significantly ahead in maintaining a healthy balance between work and life, exhibiting few, if any, imbalance symptoms. For those who have received an "AVERAGE" or "HIGH" score, I strongly encourage you to consult the recommendations I've outlined on the following page.

LOW Level of Symptoms (Score Range: 12-20): Individuals in this scoring range manage a harmonious work-life balance, effectively limiting work to conventional hours and thus preserving personal time. They generally feel rejuvenated, engaging in hobbies and relaxation without work intruding on their leisure. Their ability to disconnect from work on days off and vacations enables them to attend family and personal events consistently.

AVERAGE Level of Symptoms (Score Range: 21-29): People within this score range encounter occasional challenges in segregating their professional and private lives. Work may sporadically extend into personal time, though this isn't a constant issue. They might think about working outside office hours, occasionally struggling to allocate time for personal pursuits and self-care. They may need to postpone personal engagements due to work demands. This category encourages individuals to closely monitor their work-life balance and seek strategies to mitigate work encroachment.

HIGH Level of Symptoms (Score Range: 30-36): Individuals in this scoring range are significantly challenged in maintaining a healthy work-life balance, with work often encroaching upon personal time. This imbalance can lead to intense stress, anxiety, depression, and a higher risk of burnout. Compounding these psychological effects are unhealthy coping mechanisms, such as substance abuse (including alcohol and prescription medication addiction) and food addiction, which are particularly prevalent among those in high-stress jobs. The reliance on such coping strategies can lead to further health complications, including sleep disturbances, weight gain, and blood sugar issues.

Beyond these immediate effects, there's a social and emotional toll as individuals struggle to maintain relationships and personal well-being. It's imperative for those experiencing high levels of symptoms to undertake a serious reassessment of their work-life boundaries, explore supportive networks, and implement strategies prioritizing self-care and healthy coping mechanisms to mitigate these detrimental effects and work towards a more sustainable balance.

Chapter 2 - Checkup Recommendations

For skilled trade workers who find themselves in HIGH and AVERAGE levels of work-life imbalance symptoms, it is crucial to adopt strategies that can effectively mitigate stress, reduce burnout risk, and enhance overall well-being. Drawing from the insights provided in Chapter 2, here are tailored recommendations for each group:

For HIGH Level of Symptoms (Score Range: 30-36)

Seek Professional Support: Consider therapy or counseling to address stress, anxiety, depression, and dependency issues. Mental health professionals can provide coping strategies and support.

Establish Clear Work-Life Boundaries: Strictly delineate work hours and personal time. Make conscious efforts to disconnect from work after hours and during days off.

Prioritize Physical Health: Engage in regular physical activity, which can reduce stress and improve mental health. Also, ensure a balanced diet and adequate sleep.

Explore Healthy Coping Mechanisms: Replace unhealthy coping habits with positive ones, such as exercise, hobbies, or meditation, to manage stress without substance use or overeating.
Build a Supportive Network: Lean on friends, family, and peers for support. Sharing experiences and solutions can provide comfort and practical advice.

Time Management: Improve time management skills to enhance efficiency at work, reducing the need to extend work into personal time.

Professional Development: Engage in training or education to enhance skills, potentially reducing job-related stress and opening opportunities for less stressful positions.

Financial Planning: Address financial stressors by seeking advice on budgeting, saving, and investing to secure financial stability, which can alleviate work-related pressure.

Also, consider the recommendations for scores ranging from 21-29 for additional improvement ideas.

Chapter 2 - Checkup Recommendations

<u>For AVERAGE Level of Symptoms (Score Range: 21-29)</u>

Monitor Workload: Be vigilant about workload to prevent it from becoming overwhelming. Learn to say no or delegate tasks when possible.

Regular Breaks: Take regular breaks during work to prevent burnout and maintain productivity.
Mindfulness and Relaxation Techniques: Practice mindfulness, yoga, or meditation to manage stress effectively and maintain mental health.

Hobby and Leisure Time: Schedul that time for hobbies and activities that bring joy and relaxation, helping to detach from work stress.

Work-Life Balance Awareness: Regularly assess work-life balance and make adjustments as necessary to prevent work from increasingly encroaching on personal time.

Professional Support for Moderate Issues: Even at average levels, consulting with a mental health professional can provide strategies to manage stress and prevent escalation.

Community Engagement: Participate in community or social groups related to hobbies or interests to enhance social support and reduce isolation.

These recommendations aim to provide skilled trade workers with actionable strategies to navigate the challenges associated with high and average levels of work-life imbalance, fostering a healthier and more fulfilling personal and professional life.

<u>LOW Level of Symptoms (Score Range: 12-20)</u>

If you scored in this symptom range, keep doing what you are doing as you present lower-than-normal work-life balance symptoms. Keep in mind that life can tend to be very dynamic. As days in skilled trades roll on and stress levels at home and work go up and down, you must remain diligent in looking for imbalance symptoms.

Important note: At the beginning of each chapter in this book, you will find a QR code to access free supporting content on our website. If you ever want to retake this evaluation, you can visit this chapter's page by scanning the QR for this chapter to download blank, updated copies of this evaluation.

Chapter 3
Setting Personal and Professional Boundaries

In This Chapter

- Learn the power of "no" in professional settings

- Unveiling the truth behind the "Yes-Man" syndrome

- Discovering why "no" is your career superpower

- Evaluating the real cost of overtime in job demands

- Protecting personal and family time through boundaries

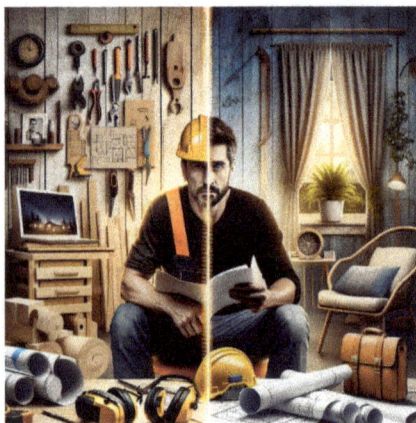

Chapter 3 focuses on setting personal and professional boundaries. It delves into the significance of saying "No" in professional settings, evaluating job demands versus overtime, and protecting personal and family time. This chapter is essential for skilled trade workers seeking a balance between their professional and personal lives, offering practical advice on managing work-related stress and prioritizing well-being.

"The difference between successful people and really successful people is that really successful people say no to almost everything."

- Warren Buffett, CEO of Berkshire Hathaway, has a Net Worth estimated at 127 Billion Dollars.

Learn more online about this chapter

Chapter 3
Setting Personal and Professional Boundaries
The power of "No" in professional settings.

Ah, the simple two-letter word **"NO."** It's short, direct, and to the point. Yet, for many, it can be the hardest word to utter, especially in a professional setting. We've all been there, drowning in a looming of responsibilities and deadlines. Yet, we still need help to decline that extra project or the invitation to yet another meeting and the elixir of solving out-of-control money problems OVERTIME. But here's the kicker: learning to say "no" is one of the most empowering things you can do for your career, mental health, and, most importantly, relationships with people in your life that matter.

The Myth of "Yes-Man" Syndrome: The corporate world, and frankly, society at large, has lionized the 'can-do' attitude. There's a pervasive belief that agreeing to everything and constantly being available are the hallmarks of a dedicated worker. Skilled trade pros who work for good companies who often display that 'can-do' spirit and know what they are doing generally find the fast lane to high wages and the most interesting work assignments, at least for a while. Here's a reality check: constantly saying "yes" will take its toll eventually. It's not a matter of if; it's a matter of when it takes its toll, as the saying goes.

Research conducted by the University of California in San Francisco found that the more difficulty one has in saying "no," the more likely they are to experience stress, burnout, and even depression. This isn't surprising, right? Spreading oneself too thin can lead to mediocre results and dissatisfaction.

As I interview trade pros on the podcast, I have noticed that for those who jump into trades right out of high school, there tends to be a longer fuse between work-life imbalance and burnout.

This crew, generally speaking, is not married, has no kids, and has high regard for making great money and the toys said money can provide. These folks can say YES to the weekend training classes, Yes to those important meetings outside normal working hours, YES to projects that require overnight travel, YES to a LOT of overtime, YES, and YES, and oh, YES!

This situation works well when a person is in their twenties and, in some cases, well into their thirties. At some point, these trade heroes' minds, bodies, or spirits will take a serious hit if the word NO is not taken out for a spin. And let's remember what happens when a boy meets a girl or vice versa.

Chapter 3
Setting Personal and Professional Boundaries
The power of "No" in professional settings.

Yes, long-lasting relationships take work, and saying YES all the to work while trying to maintain a healthy relationship rarely works.

Saying NO to the wrong things: Let's face it, our time, energy, and resources are limited. Whenever you say "yes" to one thing, many times to make your boss happy, you inadvertently say no" to something else. Think about it: if you're dedicating time to a project you're not passionate about or isn't part of your job role, you're likely saying NO to things that truly matter to you or from activities that can recharge you. Here are a few common examples I have uncovered from talking to skilled trade pros on the podcast, highlighting some of the consequences when NO is used for the wrong things.

Ripple Effect of saying Yes to work to much

Ripple ONE You are saying NO to these	Ripple TWO You are saying YES to these
Getting regular exercise.	Increase stress, Increase injury potential, General health issues.
Quality time with family and/or friends.	Feelings of isolation, loneliness, potential for substance abuse.
Quality time with wife or husband	Emotional disconnect, misunderstanding land arguments.
Quality time with children	Discipline issues, acting out, challenges at school, potential for depression.

The idea of the above table is to emphasize a ripple effect that occurs when your life is getting out of balance. Two or more ripples occur when you say YES to work too often. In the left column are common items that you are saying NO to (ripple one) when priority is placed on work. This can be for many reasons. Making more money or, as mentioned earlier, trying to stay in favor of your boss. As this water effect happens in nature, ripple one almost always leads to ripple two. In most cases, not intentionally, trade pros are saying YES to things that WILL eventually wreak havoc in their lives. NEXT UP is another anomaly that pops up when saying yes to work opportunities too often. I call this the career dilution effect that, if not recognized, can cause your career trajectory to slow as you work harder.

Chapter 3
Setting Personal and Professional Boundaries
The power of "No" in professional settings.

The career dilution effect: Besides the work-life imbalance ripple effect described on the prior page, there is another anomaly I call the **Career Dilution Effect.** This results in missed opportunities due to working too hard. Weird, right?

Here is the concept. When you possess an in-demand skillset and are in the habit of saying yes to everything, you increase the likelihood of getting assigned repetitive tasks. Being the go-to guy to get specific tasks done will get you accolades from your boss, yet could have little to no benefit to your long-term career. Think of it like an actor who gets typecast into a specific role in a popular sitcom or movie series. Despite great talent and versatility, writers and directors will cast the actor for the same role.

Let's apply the dilution effect to our skilled trade extraordinaire Otto:

Early in his career, before venturing into the entrepreneurial world, Otto excelled as a diligent tradesman. One fateful Friday afternoon, Otto's foreman, a grizzled veteran with a keen eye for talent, presented him with a lucrative offer. It was a prevailing wage project promising a generous 30% above the standard rate and all the overtime he could handle. He enthusiastically accepted, his mind already adrift in visions of a sleek new bass boat, its polished hull slicing through tranquil waters —a symbol of the rewards of his hard work and dedication.

As he delved into the project, Otto worked with the precision. Each task was executed with a finesse that made it seem like an extension of his very being. His boss, a stern but fair man, entrusting Otto with this project meant not only its timely completion but also a guarantee of exceptional quality, with minimal oversight.

An unexpected opportunity arose as the weeks turned into months on this year-long endeavor. A coveted superintendent position opened up within a company Otto had long admired. Filled with ambition, he approached his boss, only to be met with a sobering reality. Reluctantly, Otto realized the cost of his commitment as his boss politely said no, I need you to be here on the job, Otto.

This moment of realization was bittersweet. Otto understood the value of his work ethic and the trust placed in him, but it came with the sacrifice of a significant career advancement. He pondered the delicate balance between seizing the moment and planning for the future, a lesson he would carry with him as he navigated the complexities of his career path.

Chapter 3
Setting Personal and Professional Boundaries
The power of "No" in professional settings.

How do you say "NO" gracefully?: Here are some tips on how to do this while avoiding reprimands or getting fired. This, of course, assumes you are working for a good organization:

1) Be Direct but Polite: A simple "Thank you for thinking of me, but I can't commit to this right now" can be very effective.

2) Offer an Alternative: If you can't take on a project, you can suggest someone who might be interested or available.

PRO TIP: If your boss has any concerns about the person you have suggested for the job, could you offer to check in or mentor the person? This strategy can produce a win/win/win. A win for the requester. Win for the person you suggested who will most likely learn new things. Win for you in your efforts to maintain your work-life balance while avoiding career dilution.

3) Express Gratitude: If being polite is not getting the job done, a statement of appreciation may be in order. Something like, "I appreciate the offer, but I'm currently swamped with other projects, and my home life is very important to me." Please be sure to <u>BE SINCERE</u> whenever you express gratitude. This should always include a smile and eye contact.

4) Explain (if necessary): If item 1,2,3 is not enough, although you are not typically obligated to provide your boss with personal details, you may need to layer in some additional details; however, try not to share more than you need to. This is totally up to you. Whatever you do, don't lie; be sincere, and make eye contact when making your case.

Remember, saying "no" is not about being negative or unhelpful; it's about setting boundaries and ensuring you're giving your best to the tasks you commit to. So, the next time you're on the fence about another professional commitment, remember the power of "no" and use it wisely. Set your boundaries, and carry your work load in a way that fosters growth, balance, and fulfillment.

PRO TIP: Consider networking with other trade pros with whom you work. Identify other pros with similar skill levels and develop a rapport with them. The ideal situation would be to When asked to work outside normal hours, refer people to the boss. Please ask the person you referred to keep you in the loop about how the projects went. This feedback loop can give both parties a learning experience.

Chapter 3
Setting Personal and Professional Boundaries
Evaluating job demands and overtime.

The trade professional landscape has transformed tremendously. From flexible working hours to the rise of remote jobs, we are in a new era of trade work culture.

However, with this flexibility often comes the blurred line between personal and professional life. The ping of an email at 10 PM or the occasional weekend call from the boss can make one question: Where do I draw the line? Understanding the job demands and overtime is pivotal in setting clear boundaries to maintain work-life harmony.

The trade professional landscape has transformed tremendously. From flexible working hours to the rise of remote jobs, we are in a new era of trade work culture.

1. Understanding the Role and Expectations: Every job has its expectations. Some require standard working hours, while others demand more flexibility. Research from the Harvard Business Review highlighted that the ambiguity in job roles leads to overwork as employees often end up doing tasks that are more than theirs.

Over-commitment is commonly due to a need for more clarity. Before committing your precious time to any role, it's essential to understand its demands thoroughly. ALWAYS ask questions, get clarity, and know what's expected. By doing this, you can evaluate whether the overtime you're putting in is genuinely required or if you're filling in gaps due to role ambiguity.

PRO TIP: Most work activities are dynamic, meaning things change. If you choose to take on a work commitment that has the potential to include overtime, request a stipulation to have regular status discussions, especially at the front end of the assignment. Start with weekly discussion and adjust as needed. When committing, express how many overtime hours you can commit if needed. If the job requirements trend towards exceeding your commitment, try to get an agreement in advance that help will be provided to get overtime hours back in line with the commitment.

2. The Real Cost of Overtime: Let's talk numbers. According to a study by Stanford University, employee productivity starts to decline after 50 hours of work in a week, and anyone putting in 70 hours produces about 55 hours of additional work output, NOT 70. It's not just about diminishing returns in terms of output; there's a mental cost. Overwork leads to burnout, increased stress levels, health issues, and the potential for job site injuries. So, while working that extra hour adds value, it could be doing more harm than good.

Chapter 3
Setting Personal and Professional Boundaries
Evaluating job demands and overtime.

3. Work Smart, Not Just Hard: It's not just about the hours you put in but the efficiency with which you work. You can use tools and technologies that can help streamline tasks. The Pareto Principle, or the 80/20 rule, suggests that 80% of results come from 20% of efforts. Focus on tasks that yield maximum results and consider delegating or dropping tasks that eat up time without substantial returns.

4. Regular Check-ins and Adjustments: The work culture and personal demands are dynamic, so it's essential to reassess and adjust your work-life balance regularly. This might involve periodic check-ins with yourself (self-reflection) or your boss about your workload, work hours, and the impact on your personal life, as we covered earlier in this chapter. Being proactive about making adjustments can help prevent burnout and ensure your professional and personal needs are met effectively.

5. Embracing Flexibility Wisely: While flexible working hours and remote work options offer great advantages, they require disciplined time management. Embracing flexibility means adapting your work schedule to fit your life's demands while ensuring productivity. It's crucial to distinguish between being flexibly available and being perpetually on-call. You can use the flexibility to create a schedule that allows you to be productive while attending to your needs and responsibilities.

6. Prioritizing Personal Well-being: Personal well-being should not be sacrificed for career growth. Investing time in self-care, hobbies, and relationships is essential. Activities like regular exercise, hobbies, and spending time with loved ones are crucial for maintaining a healthy work-life balance. This balance improves mental and physical health and enhances productivity and job satisfaction, allowing for a fulfilling career without compromising personal life.

The importance of continually assessing job demands and the necessity for overtime cannot be overstated. As industries evolve and work environments become even more dynamic, adapting and re-evaluating one's work commitments is paramount. Passion and dedication to one's career are indeed qualities to be admired. However, it is crucial to remember that work constitutes only a single facet of our lives. In striving for excellence in our professional endeavors, we must remember the other elements contributing to a fulfilling life.

Establishing and maintaining clear boundaries between our personal and professional lives is essential for several reasons. Firstly, it allows individuals to achieve work-life balance, which is fundamental to long-term professional success.

Chapter 3
Setting Personal and Professional Boundaries
Protecting personal and family time

The Need for Boundaries: A study by the American Psychological Association (APA) found that people who don't establish clear boundaries between work and personal time experience higher stress levels and are at risk for burnout.

The Benefits of Protecting Personal and Family Time: Carving out and protecting personal and family time has numerous benefits. For one, it strengthens our relationships. Quality time spent with loved ones helps build stronger bonds and understanding. Furthermore, taking time off from work provides an opportunity for rest and rejuvenation, which boosts productivity when we return to our tasks.

Remember that time spent with family isn't just good for the soul; it's also essential for our brain. According to research from the University of California, Irvine, downtime, like engaging in leisure activities with family or simply resting, is essential for the brain's processing, allowing it to make sense of experiences and solidify memories.

Boundaries protecting your homelife

1. Set Specific Times: Just as you schedule meetings, set specific times for family activities and personal relaxation. It could be the dinner hour, where no phones are allowed, or a weekend morning walk.

2. Technology Detox: Consider having "phone-free" zones at home or "unplugged" hours when no electronic devices are used. This not only reduces distractions but also helps foster genuine connections.

3. Communication is Key: Inform your colleagues and boss about your boundaries. They know why and when you would like to hear back from you if you don't answer calls, texts, or emails after 6 PM. Most professionals will respect these boundaries once they are communicated, which will help reduce stress for your teammates.

4. Learn to Say No: This might be tough, especially if you're a people-pleaser. However, I'd like to point out that declining additional tasks or commitments that interfere with your time is necessary.

Setting Personal and Professional Boundaries
Protecting personal and family time

5. Reevaluate Regularly: As life changes—whether because of a new job, the birth of a child, or any number of reasons—so will the nature of our boundaries. Check in with yourself periodically to ensure your drawn lines make sense.

6. Reflect and Adjust Regularly: Set aside time each month to review your boundaries. Are they serving their purpose? Are there new stressors or life changes that require adjustment? This reflection ensures that your boundaries evolve with your life's changing needs.

7. Practice Assertiveness: Develop a calm, clear way of communicating your needs. This might involve role-playing with a trusted friend or learning phrases that comfortably express your boundaries. Remember, it's not just about what you say but how you say it.

8. Avoid Overcommitting: Learn to evaluate your availability realistically before taking on new commitments. This might involve checking your calendar before agreeing to new projects or social engagements. Overcommitting leads to stress and burnout, making it harder to maintain boundaries.

9. Understand Your Limits: Spend introspection to understand what you can realistically handle. This may involve recognizing your emotional, physical, and mental limits. Knowing these helps set boundaries that protect your well-being without causing unnecessary friction.

10. Delegate Tasks: Identify tasks at work or home that others can handle. This could involve training a colleague at work or your kids at home to take over certain responsibilities or sharing household chores with family members. Delegating effectively frees up your time and energy for higher-priority tasks and self-care.

11. The Power of Modeling: If you're in a leadership position, remember that setting boundaries isn't just for your well-being; it's also about modeling healthy behaviors for your team. When employees see their leaders respecting and valuing personal and family time, they are likelier to do the same, leading to a more balanced and happier workforce.

Setting Personal and Professional Boundaries

Otto and Carol – The transformation begins: In the months following Otto's accident, new beginnings for Otto and Carol started to take hold. Slowly, together, Carol and Otto began reopening lines of communication that had been absent from their marriage for many years.

Otto finally agreed to attend couples marriage counseling, resulting in ways to communicate with each other in a more caring and measured tone. Not surprisingly, their twin boys seem to argue and fight a little less.

Over time, Otto also learned new tools to take in what his wife was trying to share without feeling attacked. For the first time in his working life, he started measuring the real costs to his family and other important relationships when he was always working so much. He also started taking inventory of his health, both physically and mentally.

Over several months, Otto gradually delegated dealing with fires that came up during the day, clawing back personal time to spend with Carol, the boys, and friends he had lost touch with.

At first, Otto's longtime customers and business partners pushed back. Otto was the go-to guy for a long time when problems popped up in the business. As Otto got better at saying no, opportunities for younger leaders in his company to step up, and Otto was okay with that. During normal working hours, Otto's role evolved from a go-to guy to more of a mentor to the younger future leaders of the business, and it felt good.

Otto's partners and the company leadership team started to see Otto in a new light. Not being around outside working hours as much resulted in Otto's time being less diluted, and, for the first time, his value to the company began to expand from being just the go to when problems came up.

As folks around him got more comfortable with how the company could still function without Otto being there 60 hours a week, Otto started to enjoy A LOT more flexibility in his work hours. He could even work from home a few days a week if he chose to.

Although Otto's new work life initially felt awkward, he felt encouraged. Learning to say no and deligating was a major step in his transformation. His next big step was to take control of his time.

Chapter 3
Setting Personal and Professional Boundaries

1) Learn to Say 'No': Practice assertiveness professionally. Understand that saying 'no' to excessive work demands is essential for maintaining your health and personal life. It helps in setting clear boundaries and prevents burnout.

2) Evaluate Your Workload: Regularly assess your job demands. If you're consistently working overtime or taking work home, discussing workload management with your supervisor might be time.

3) Protect Personal and Family Time: Deliberately schedule time for personal activities and family. Treat these commitments with the same importance as professional meetings to ensure a balanced life.

4) Develop Assertive Communication Skills: Improve how you communicate boundaries to colleagues and superiors. Assertive communication is key to setting and maintaining these boundaries without negative repercussions.

5) Seek Support When Needed: Don't hesitate to seek support from HR, a mentor, or a counselor if you struggle to balance work and personal life. Sometimes, external guidance can provide new perspectives and strategies.

"Focus is not saying yes to the thing you've got to focus on. It's saying no to the hundred other good ideas that there are. You have to pick carefully."

-Steve Jobs, Co-Founder, Apple Computers

Chapter 4
Time Management for the Tradesperson

In This Chapter

- Challenges of over-reliance on technology and information overload.

- Constant connectivity impacts tradespeople's personal time.

- Keeping up with rapid technological advancements and cybersecurity.

- Traditional work practices cause inefficiencies.

- Integrating effective habits into both professional and personal life.

Chapter 4 covers critical aspects of time management for tradespeople. It unpacks their unique challenges in today's high-tech world, where technology-based distractions vie for their attention, impacting work-life balance. The chapter also revisits the perennial time traps inherent in old-school skilled trades, emphasizing the constant battle against time for tradespeople.

With an engaging narrative, it highlights the pervasive allure of technology and its impact on productivity. It also offers practical time management strategies that resonate with the tradesperson's daily reality. These insights empower tradespeople to navigate demanding schedules more effectively, ensuring a balanced approach to their professional and personal lives.

"It's not enough to be busy, so are the ants. The question is, what are we busy about?"

– Henry David Thoreau, American essayist, poet, philosopher,

Learn more online about this chapter

Chapter 4
Time Management for the Tradesperson

Challenges in this high-tech world.

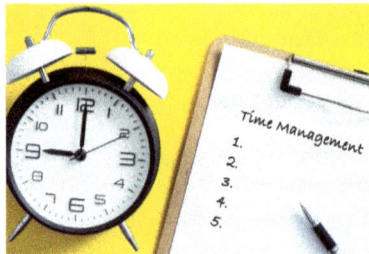

Do these numbers (39,045,600 and 42,573,600) mean anything to you? Or, how about the saying, life is temporary? These two numbers represent the number of minutes men and women live in America, respectively. Surprising yes/no?

Regardless of our gene pool and how we treat our bodies and minds as we travel through life, we only have a finite amount of time on this earth, so how we manage our time matters A LOT. Time management is likely the most important skill we can gain. Unfortunately, most people learn time management out of necessity long after graduating from high school, if at all. What a shame it is that our kids can have the capacity to understand time at a very young age, yet they receive little education about its importance or how to manage it smartly.

In contrast, I want to acknowledge that spontaneity also has its place in our daily lives. Having the free will to make our own choices regarding how we spend our time is indeed one of the blessings of the human experience. Yes, hanging on to those impromptu moments, especially in family life, is important and must be protected and cherished. As we move into this chapter, time management and spontaneity can cohabitate. In many respects, balancing reasonable time management with spontaneity is a key component to living a balanced, productive life.

Let's start by looking at some of the challenges that skilled trade pros are dealing with that can make time management especially challenging:

1. Over-reliance on Technology: One of the primary challenges in this digital age is the tendency to over-rely on technology. While tools like project management software and mobile apps can enhance work efficiency, they can also create a false sense of security. The danger lies in assuming technology will handle all aspects at lightning speed. The downside of over-reliance on technology is that your brilliantly laid-out plans can also EXPLODE at lightning speed.

2. Information Overload: The sheer volume of information available can be overwhelming. Email notifications, digital tool alerts, and online resources constantly vying for attention make concentrating on the task difficult. This information overload can lead to decision fatigue, decreased productivity, and increased stress levels.

Chapter 4
Time Management for the Tradesperson

Challenges in this high-tech world.

3. Constant Connectivity: Blurred the lines between work and personal life. Tradespeople often find themselves always "on call," leading to burnout, reduced efficiency, and eventually to work-life imbalance. Because of accelerating workforce shortages, these challenges are more common for trade pros than white-collar occupations.

4. Keeping Up with Technological Advancements: Technology advancement for products and services that skilled trade pros interact with was slower than in the rest of the digital age. As a result, the technology embedded in products and used to service products has been playing catch up.

5. Cybersecurity Concerns: Increased reliance on digital tools comes with the risk of cybersecurity threats. Time spent dealing with cyber-attacks or data breaches can significantly disrupt work schedules and project timelines. Trades pros have been on a crash course to keep up with the cat and mouse that came with cyber security again, more so than white-collar occupations.

6. Task Automation and Delegation: While technology offers opportunities for automation, deciding what and when to automate can be challenging. Over-automation can lead to losing personal touch and craftsmanship in the trade.

7. Digital Distractions: The temptation of digital distractions like social media and online content is ever-present. These distractions can chip away at valuable work time, leading to delayed projects, increased stress, and eventually lead to the destruction of work-life balance.

While the high-tech world offers numerous tools for improving time management, it also brings several challenges that tradespeople need to navigate. Effective time management in this era is not just about using the right tools; it's about integrating them into work practices to enhance productivity without compromising the quality of work or personal well-being. Adapting to these challenges requires a combination of technological savvy, disciplined work habits, and continuous learning.

Next, we will look at the most common time traps rooted in the application of technology. Recognizing these traps can be a significant step forward in maintaining a work-life balance.

Chapter 4
Time Management for the Tradesperson
Technology-based Time traps and their impact on work-life balance.

Technology is here to stay despite its challenges and has given rise to a new set of challenges known as technology-based time traps. These traps particularly affect skilled trades workers, significantly Impacting their work-life balance.

Data is a double-edged sword: On one hand, tools like email, instant messaging, and project management apps have streamlined many aspects of work, making it easier to communicate and coordinate. This looks great on the surface. Regarding trades, these distractions, if not managed smartly, create scheduling nightmares when pros get bogged down with the "Got a Minute" calls. These Got a Minute calls generally go out to a company's most experienced, highest-paid pros, leading to significant inefficiencies if not managed smartly.

The administrative nightmare: Another technology-based time trap is the increased administrative burden of digital systems. While technology has automated many administrative tasks, it has also introduced new ones. Trades workers, especially those who run their own businesses, now manage digital records, input data into various software systems, and navigate online platforms for tasks like invoicing, processing customer payments, scheduling, and procurement. This additional administrative workload can eat into working and personal time, diminishing the time available for rest and leisure.

Time for an update: The rapid pace of technological change is another time trap. Skilled trades workers must continually update their technical knowledge and adapt to new tools and technologies. This necessity for ongoing education and training often requires personal time, which can detract from time spent with family or other personal interests.

Moreover, integrating AI and IoT devices in workplace operations necessitates a higher level of technical proficiency from workers, further blurring the lines between traditional trades and technology roles. As these systems become more complex and interconnected, the demand for skilled technicians who can troubleshoot, upgrade, and maintain them increases. This evolution in job requirements pressures workers to continually update their skills and places them in a cycle of perpetual learning. Consequently, the mental and emotional strain of keeping pace with technological advancements can add another layer of stress, compounding the challenge of achieving a balanced life amidst the demands of modern trade professions.

Chapter 4
Time Management for the Tradesperson
Technology-based Time traps and their impact on work-life balance.

Did you see that cat video?: Social media and online distractions represent a double-edged sword in the context of modern skilled trades. On one hand, platforms like YouTube offer invaluable resources for learning new skills, staying updated on industry trends, and even troubleshooting unusual problems encountered on the job.

The potential for professional growth and community building through these channels must be considered. However, the lure of engaging yet ultimately unproductive content is strong. The cat video mentioned earlier is just one example of the myriad distractions that can consume far more time than intended.

The phenomenon isn't limited to just browsing social media. The proliferation of instant messaging apps and email notifications means workers are constantly bombarded with potential distractions. While staying connected is crucial, the constant interruptions can fragment attention and significantly decrease productivity.

Some organizations are taking proactive steps to combat these issues. Training sessions emphasizing the importance of digital literacy, including the ability to assess the value of online content concerning professional development critically, are becoming more common. Workshops on time management strategies that incorporate the judicious use of technology are also gaining traction. These educational initiatives are complemented by workplace policies designed to minimize unnecessary digital distractions. For example, some job sites may restrict access to certain websites or apps during work hours, except for designated breaks.

Ultimately, the key to navigating the pitfalls of online distractions lies in cultivating a disciplined approach to technology use. By setting personal limits, utilizing tools that monitor or restrict app usage, and prioritizing tasks, trade workers can reclaim much of the time lost to digital distractions. Employers, for their part, can support these efforts by creating an environment that values productivity and well-being in equal measure. Through combined efforts, it's possible to harness the benefits of technology without falling prey to its more time-consuming traps, ensuring that skilled tradespeople remain productive, satisfied, and balanced in their professional and personal lives.

Chapter 4
Time Management for the Tradesperson
Old-school Skilled Trades time traps, that are never going away

Old school can also be a problem: Tech-based time traps are just one web trade workers can find themselves in. Deeply ingrained in the ethos and operations of various trades, they manifest in various non-technological aspects. You may have experienced some of these at your place of employment.

Rigid Hierarchies in Work Culture: Skilled trades often operate within firmly established hierarchical structures, where experience and time in the trade dictate authority and decision-making power. This hierarchy, while valuable for maintaining quality and safety standards, can become a time trap when it stifles the voices of less experienced workers who may have innovative ideas or more efficient methods of working. The extent of challenges in this area is highly dependent on company culture. Some companies encourage team members from all experience levels to speak up, and some do not.

Manual Processes and Paperwork: Despite advancements in other areas, many trades still rely heavily on manual processes for administrative tasks like job tracking, invoicing, and inventory management. The reliance on physical paperwork can be a significant time trap, leading to inefficiencies in communication, delays in project timelines, and increased potential for errors.

Traditional Apprenticeship Lengths and Rigid Training: Apprenticeships in skilled trades are known for their length and rigor, often lasting several years. While this ensures a high level of skill and knowledge, it can also act as a time trap, especially when the training rigidly adheres to traditional timelines and methods, regardless of an individual's learning pace or prior experience.

Resistance to Process Innovation: Even without considering technology, many trades are characterized by resistance to change in processes or methods. This conservatism, often rooted in a "that's how it's always been done" mindset, can be a significant time trap, as it prevents exploring potentially more efficient or effective ways of completing tasks.

Inflexible Work Schedules: The traditional 9-to-5 work schedule, often with strict start and end times, is common in many trades. This inflexibility can become a time trap, especially when it doesn't align with the most efficient or productive times for workers or doesn't accommodate the fluctuating nature of some projects.

Time Management for the Tradesperson
Old-school Skilled Trades time traps, that are never going away

Hard on the body: In skilled trades, focusing too much on traditional physical skills often overlooks the benefits of ergonomics, leading to various workplace problems. While it's important to respect old methods, ignoring ergonomic practices that improve safety and efficiency can result in more fatigue and slower work. Over time, this can lead to long-term health problems for workers, increasing absences and staff turnover. Putting too much emphasis on physical strength without thinking about ergonomic improvements can make everyday tasks dangerous, reducing the productivity and health of workers overall.

Bad COMS: The issue of communication gaps and mismanagement further complicates the landscape of skilled trades. Despite the critical role of effective communication in ensuring smooth operations and safety, entrenched hierarchical structures often create barriers. These barriers prevent essential information from flowing freely between management and frontline workers. The result is a work environment where feedback and insights, which could significantly improve processes and safety protocols, are stifled. This lack of open dialogue breeds inefficiencies and delays and contributes to a culture of misunderstanding and frustration, undermining team cohesion and morale.

Limited to no cross-training: While deep expertise in a particular area is invaluable, the absence of a more diversified skill set among workers limits the team's ability to adapt to changing circumstances or to efficiently redistribute tasks during peak periods or when facing unforeseen challenges. This rigidity in skill allocation not only affects the immediate responsiveness of the team but also hampers long-term strategic flexibility, making it difficult for organizations to navigate the evolving demands of their industries. Dedication to a cross-training program within old-school organizations is essential to combat these challenges.

Recognizing and addressing these old-school issues is crucial for the sustainability and growth of any organization within the skilled trades. It requires a commitment from management to acknowledge existing shortcomings and to invest in comprehensive strategies aimed at promoting ergonomic practices, enhancing communication channels, and encouraging cross-training. Such initiatives improve the immediate working conditions and productivity of the workforce and contribute to building a more resilient and adaptable organization capable of thriving in an ever-changing economic landscape.

Chapter 4
Time Management for the Tradesperson
BIG MONEY after your eyeballs

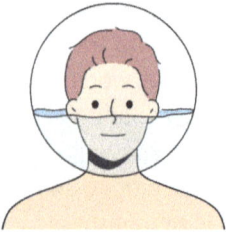

Stephan R. Covey, author of The Seven Habits of Highly Effective People, says, "Be careful not to get caught up in the thick of thin things." Translation: without structure to how you spend your time, it is easy to spend WAY too much time thinking about or doing things that have little to no benefit to achieving your goals. A good example of getting caught up in the thick of thin things is social media.

Now, wait, I know. Yes, there is value to social media. These amazing technologies make it possible to keep in touch with friends, learn stuff, and watch a cat video or two that will make you smile.

Question: Have you ever started surfing YouTube, Facebook, Instagram, or TikTok and lost track of time? This is **NOT AN ACCIDENT.**

Just how big is social media? In 2023, worldwide gross revenue for all major social platforms was estimated to be over $225 billion, and it is projected to reach $263 billion by 2028. Yes, this is BIG MONEY! Before we look further into time management, let's do some math that should give you additional perspective into the value of your time and how social media can be one of life's biggest time thieves in modern times.

Like most things in life, free is not free. Folks at these high-tech companies are getting paid VERY WELL to keep users like you engaged (ideally addicted) with these social platforms. Marketers know that millions of eyeballs engrossed on these platforms are money-making units. Yes, others are VERY SMART people working at these platforms who use every tool possible to make these platforms as addicting as possible.

How much time do you think we're talking about? Since I am a simple man, we will look at one week out of the 52 weeks in a year. A week is seven days, and we all get 24 hours per day. This puts our total hours at (24 x 7) 168 per week. Most skilled trade pros work about 9 hours per day, five days per week; this comes to about 45 hours per week. So, 45 hours / 168 per our total work hours is about 27% of our available time. This puts the amount of time we are not working at about 123 hours or 73%.

Question: How much of the approximate 73% of your hours not working are spent on social media or watching TV? Data on the next page may shock you.

Chapter 4
Time Management for the Tradesperson
BIG MONEY after your eyeballs

This graphic is based on data from the US Bureau of Labor Statistics, breaking down what Americans spend time on over their lifetime. Between using social media and watching TV, the average American spends over **FIFTEEN YEARS** engaged. No wonder these platforms place a high value on getting our eyeballs locked on and, ideally, addicted. Every hour Americans can claw back will result in a dramatic improvement in the work-life balance equation.

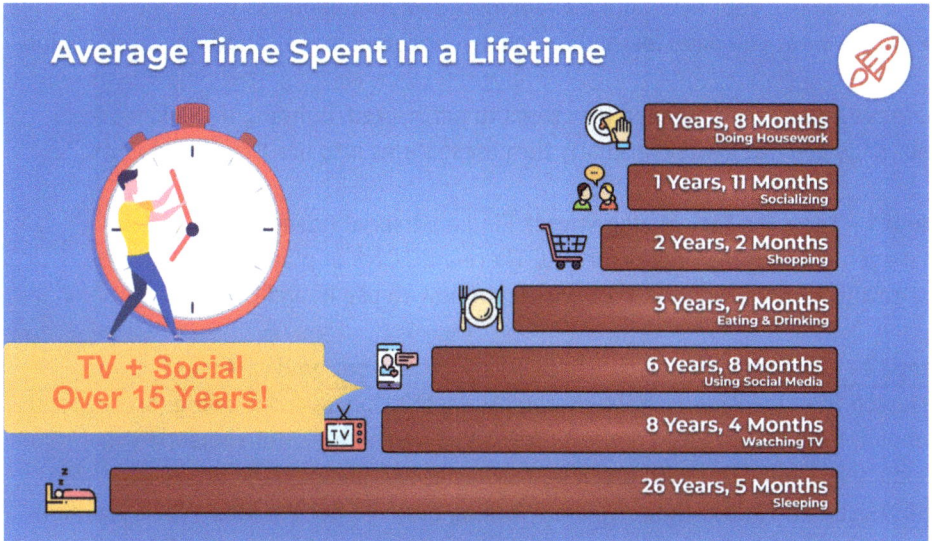

Average Time Spent In a Lifetime

1 Years, 8 Months	Doing Housework
1 Years, 11 Months	Socializing
2 Years, 2 Months	Shopping
3 Years, 7 Months	Eating & Drinking
6 Years, 8 Months	Using Social Media
8 Years, 4 Months	Watching TV
26 Years, 5 Months	Sleeping

TV + Social Over 15 Years!

Employers are responding: Employers face a silent battle against social media distractions, eroding workplace productivity and safety. The stakes are higher in skilled trades, where glancing at a phone can lead to serious accidents, from auto mishaps to slips on construction sites. These distractions diminish productivity and inflate insurance costs, presenting a dual challenge for businesses. The quest for a solution spans from promoting digital mindfulness in offices to emphasizing safety and the consequences of inattention among tradespeople.

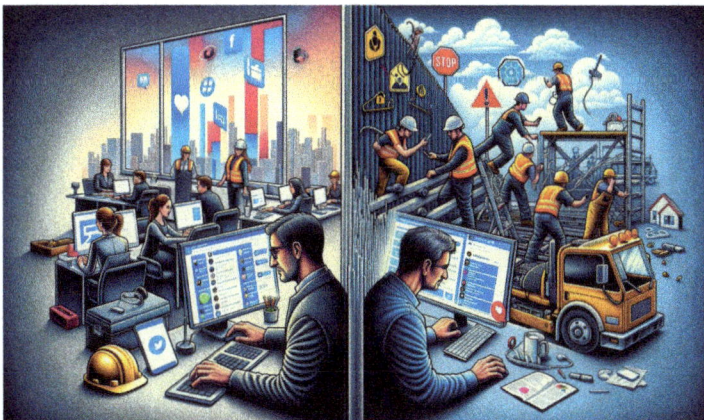

Chapter 4
Time Management for the Tradesperson
Time management concepts that work.

With an understanding of the challenges, time traps, and the impact of TV social media on work-life balance, let's look at some time management concepts that can help dramatically in your personal and professional life:

- Create a system to manage your time better.
- Identify your time traps.
- You can use your new time management system to address your time traps.
- Apply what you have learned to boost your career and strengthen relationships.

Here are some recommended first steps to get started. Building these steps into your daily activities will eventually turn these items into life-changing habits :

Step#1 - Tools for Task Management: Find a personal (ideally mobile) time management tool that works for you. There are TONS of platforms out there, especially for smartphones. Pick one, learn how to use it, and USE IT!

Step#2 - Block time: Block-timing tasks aren't new but golden. According to research from the American Psychological Association, task-switching (or constantly jumping from one task to another) can cost as much as 40% of someone's productive Time. Start with blocking the basics like Sleep, Work hours, Time with wife/husband, Time with Kid(s), and Working out; you get the idea. When you block out Time, BE REALISTIC. For example, if you attend your kid('s) baseball game, your time block should include drive time and this before you leave work "Got-A-Minute" request as you are trying to walk out the door.

HELPFUL TIPS

PRO TIP: Block time is seldom perfect, so try not to beat up on yourself when you mess up.

Step#3 - Set a Goal within your Block time: You have blocked out time in your time management tool. Your first block time is **"Spend quality time at home."** Now what? Although this is a great first step, you must set a goal for this (and all) periods you block out.

In this example, simply improving your time management skills must include the outcome you are trying to achieve. So, in this example, your block time with the **"Spend quality time at home."** could contain the following goals: **1. Get home by 5:15 PM at least three days a week.   2. I will spend one-on-one time with my wife and kids. 3. I will research potential non-work-related hobbies that I would like to pick up and block additional time to get started.** Just to let you know, there are many ways to do this step. The overall objective for stating goals within your block times is to -->

Time Management for the Tradesperson

Time management concepts that work.

--> get a clear picture of what successful progress or completion looks like. As with the example provided here, some tasks are repetitive so that these block times will stay active on your time management tool indefinitely, and that's OK. In these cases, you will update goals and to-dos that are coming up next.

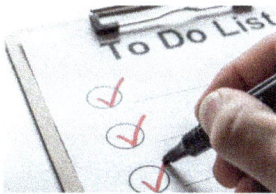

Step#4 - Connecting to-dos to your goals: Effectively managing your time involves a crucial process: connecting your daily to-dos directly to your goals. Once you've allocated a specific block of time in your schedule for a goal, it's essential to explain clearly why you're dedicating time to this objective to justify your commitment. The subsequent step is to meticulously compile a list of to-dos necessary for attaining your goal. This list can vary greatly in length and detail depending on the nature of the goal. For simpler, short-term objectives, your to-do list might be brief and straightforward, encompassing activities that can be completed within a single time block. Conversely, more complex and long-term goals, such as completing an apprenticeship program, require a more comprehensive list of activities, possibly spread over several weeks, months, or even years.

When constructing your to-do list, you must conduct thorough research and planning to ensure that all necessary steps are included. This involves breaking down larger goals into smaller, more manageable to-dos, making the overall objective less daunting and more achievable.

As you work towards your goals, remaining flexible and adaptive is also important. Goals and priorities can change as new information emerges or as you make progress in your to-do's. You may find that certain to-dos require more time than initially anticipated, or new to-dos that should have been considered at the outset might emerge. Therefore, regularly reviewing and adjusting your to-do list is critical to stay aligned with your goals. Despite these adjustments, the primary focus should always be on consistently progressing toward achieving your goal. By keeping your to-dos directly linked to your goals and adapting your plan as necessary, you can maintain a clear direction and enhance your overall productivity and effectiveness in managing your time.

HELPFUL TIPS

PRO TIP (for to-do lists): Try to batch similar tasks whenever possible. For example, you have two home improvement tasks on your to-do list to finish, and both are repairing electrical

Chapter 4
Time Management for the Tradesperson
Time management concepts that work.

Employer-paid learning (Skilled Trade Hack): Millions of skilled trade workers are on the road on any given day, driving from one job site to the next. These minutes and, in many cases, hours of windshield time are generally paid for by your company and, ultimately, by the customer. Consider blocking time to listen to audiobooks and personal or career-enhancing podcasts. While engaged in windshield time, provided that your work activities are all caught up, time spent doing self-improvement while getting paid is golden. **NEVER, EVER, EVER, EVER** engage in distracted driving. You must ALWAYS be safe while driving. You can always check out your company employee manual (or ask) to find out if you're not listening to content while driving, which is NOT a violation of company policy.

Otto and Carol - Getting back on track with time management: Otto has been in his new role for about six months. During that time, his company sent him to specialized training that was very handy. One of his classes covered using the company's time management software, and, for the first time, he had a place to keep track of his personal and work commitments using block time.

Once he mastered his work calendar, he picked a time management calendar that he, Carol, and eventually the boys started to use together. Who would have thought that by diligently using some time management tools and learning how to use them, Otto and his family could start getting their life back? The next time we check in on these two, we will find out how Otto chooses to deal with years of abusing his body while working in skilled trades.

In "Atomic Habits," James Clear champions small, incremental changes to build good habits, emphasizing systems over goals for long-term success. His Four Laws of Behavior Change—make it obvious, attractive, easy, and satisfying—offer a framework particularly applicable to time management. By breaking tasks into smaller steps (easy), setting clear reminders (obvious), rewarding task completion (attractive), and providing immediate positive feedback (satisfying), individuals can improve their productivity. Integrating these principles into time management strategies helps cultivate disciplined, efficient approaches to scheduling and task execution. This methodology simplifies time management and ensures that improvements are impactful and enduring, leading to greater overall personal and professional satisfaction.

Check out the resourced pages at the back of this book for information on "Atomic Habits" by James Clear and other resources to help you find and maintain work-life balance while working in skilled trades.

Chapter 4 - Checkup

In Chapter 1, we explored the general state of your work-life balance. Then, after finishing Chapter 2, we pinpointed the most frequent symptoms of an unbalanced lifestyle. As we wrap up this chapter, we will perform another checkup on **time management**. Recognizing this skill, which must be cultivated, is crucial because it balances our professional responsibilities and personal lives.

Instructions

As we delve into this critical checkpoint in our journey through understanding and improving our time management skills, let's take a moment to prepare adequately for this assessment. Following these instructions will help you gain the most from this self-evaluation.

Set Up Your Space

Find a Quiet Area: Choose a location where you're least likely to be interrupted. This could be a serene room in your home or a peaceful outdoor setting. The goal is to have a comfortable space conducive to deep thought.

Eliminate Distractions: Turn off notifications on all your devices to avoid interruptions. Please let those around you know that this assessment will not disturb you. This time is for you, and minimizing distractions is key.

Ensure Comfort: Make sure your chosen spot has adequate lighting and seating. Comfortable surroundings will help maintain focus and prevent physical discomfort from distracting you during the assessment.

Choose the Right Time

Timing Is Key: Schedule your assessment when most alert and relaxed. This is often in the morning, within the first two hours after waking up. Avoid scheduling this during or immediately after work hours, as fatigue or stress may influence your responses.

Prepare Your Mind and Body: Engage in light exercise or meditation before starting. These activities can help clear your mind, reduce stress, and create a positive self-assessment tone.

Responding to Questions

Be honest: I'd like you to approach this assessment as an opportunity for self-reflection. There are no right or wrong answers here, only honest reflections on your current state of time management. Your openness and honesty are crucial for an accurate self-evaluation. --->

Chapter 4 - Checkup

Instructions
- Responding to Questions Continued -

First Instincts: Trust your gut reaction to each question. Your initial response usually reflects your true feelings and circumstances. Please don't worry about overthinking your answers.

Don't Dwell on One Question: If you are hesitating on a question, take it as a sign to move on. Spending too much time on one question can hinder the assessment flow and may not yield more accurate insights.

Take A Moment

Taking a moment to center yourself before tackling the checkup is not just a preliminary step; it's crucial to ensure you approach this introspective exercise with the clarity and calm it requires. Setting aside the whirlwind of daily tasks and concerns creates a mental space primed for reflection—a key to unlocking deeper insights into your time management habits. This preparatory pause is a gateway to a more focused and meaningful engagement with the questions ahead.

Lastly, I'd like you to approach this evaluation with a spirit of openness and curiosity and let it catalyze positive change. This is your journey towards mastering the art of time management, paving the way for a lifestyle that aligns with your highest aspirations and values. Let's embrace this process with enthusiasm and an eagerness for the self-improvement that lies ahead, and THERE ARE NO right or wrong answers here.

If your scoring indicates areas for improvement, I will make some recommendations before proceeding with the next chapter.

Chapter 4 - Checkup

Step 1: Read each scenario in the left column. Then, circle a 1, 2, or 3 if...............

1 = RARELY happens | 2 = Happens ONCE IN A WHILE | 3 = Happens ALL THE TIME.

Step 2: Once you have scored each item, write your "Your total Score: >" at the bottom of the page in the box provided.

1) How often do you struggle with prioritizing tasks?		1	2	3
2) How frequently do you find yourself missing deadlines, necessitating overtime or impinging on personal time?		1	2	3
3) How regularly do you forego breaks, potentially leading to burnout or decreased productivity?		1	2	3
4) How often do distractions, particularly from digital devices, significantly disrupt your focus?		1	2	3
5) How frequently does technology usage become a procrastination tool rather than a productivity enhancer?		1	2	3
6) How often are work interruptions a major hindrance to maintaining a steady workflow?		1	2	3
7) How regularly do you neglect setting aside time for learning new skills or technologies, affecting your work efficiency?		1	2	3
8) How frequently do you fail to maintain clear boundaries between work and personal life, allowing work to intrude on personal time?		1	2	3
9) How often do communication tools become more of a complication than a solution in your work processes?		1	2	3
10) How frequently do you miss opportunities to automate tasks, leading to unnecessary time spent on repetitive work?		1	2	3
11) How often do you fail to plan and schedule effectively, resulting in a poor balance between work and personal activities?		1	2	3
12) How regularly do you overlook evaluating and adjusting your time management strategies, hindering improvement?		1	2	3
Your Total Score ---	>>			

Chapter 4 - Checkup

After reviewing your assessment results, please take a moment to acknowledge the significance of your score. If your score is within the "Optimal" range, it signifies your effective time management skills in balancing work and personal life with minimal signs of imbalance. For those with scores in the "Moderate" or "Challenged" categories, consider the strategies outlined to enhance your work-life balance, specifically improving time management between professional obligations and personal life.

Optimal Time Management (Score 12-20): This score signifies excellent work and personal time management, with individuals successfully delineating between their professional responsibilities and personal lives. They manage to keep work within designated hours, allowing ample personal time for rejuvenation and leisure activities. These individuals are proficient in disengaging from work during their downtime, including vacations and weekends, thereby maintaining attendance at family and personal events without work interference. Continuous mindfulness is recommended to preserve this balance. If your score outcome was optimal, that is excellent. I recommend you look at the recommendations on the next page, as some of the recommendations presented may still be beneficial to you.

Moderate Time Management (Score 21-29): Those within this scoring bracket experience occasional difficulties maintaining a clear division between work and personal life. Work may sometimes spill over into personal time, but it is not a pervasive problem. There might be instances where work preoccupies their thoughts outside work hours, leading to challenges in dedicating time to personal interests and self-care. Occasionally, work demands may necessitate the postponement of personal activities. It is advisable for individuals in this category to actively monitor their time management practices and explore strategies to prevent work from increasingly encroaching on personal time.

Challenged Time Management (Score 30-36): Individuals scoring in this range face significant challenges in managing their time effectively between work and personal life, with work frequently impinging upon personal time. This imbalance can result in elevated stress levels, the potential for burnout, and a reliance on unhealthy coping mechanisms. The extensive hours spent on work commitments often lead to missing out on personal and family activities. Individuals with high scores are urged to critically reassess their time management strategies, seeking support and adopting measures to prioritize self-care and establish a healthier work-life balance.

Chapter 4 - Checkup Recommendations

For individuals navigating the complexities of time management within skilled trades, the results of this evaluation offer insightful guidance. Suppose your final score reflects higher frequencies of time management challenges. In that case, it underscores the need for proactive steps to build on your time management skills, reduce work-related stress, and foster a healthier work-life integration. Below, I have included some recommendations to help you improve.

<u>Challenged Time Management (Score 30-36)</u>

Embracing Technology Wisely: Use Technology to your advantage, but avoid falling into "technology-based time traps." Apps and digital tools should streamline the time management process.

Blocking your time: We covered setting aside a block of time earlier in this chapter. Time-blocking goals and tasks into an easy-to-use tool, especially tools that are easily accessible, can help improve your entire time management landscape.

Prioritizing Tasks: Focus on what's truly important. This involves understanding which tasks are urgent and important and which can wait. It's essential to distinguish between tasks needing immediate attention and those less critical.

Setting Realistic Goals: Set achievable goals within reasonable timelines to avoid the stress of overcommitment. Breaking down larger projects into manageable tasks can help make steady progress without feeling overwhelmed.

Self-Care and Downtime: Prioritize self-care by ensuring you have downtime for relaxation and activities you enjoy, vital for maintaining a good work-life balance and reducing burnout risk.

Microlearning Strategy: Adopt a microlearning approach to skill enhancement, particularly in time management. Learn best time management practices and put these concepts to work in your world cost-effectively.

Feedback and Adjustment: Please always seek feedback on your time management strategies and be willing to adjust your approach based on what is working and what isn't. Continuous improvement in time management practices can lead to more effective work-life integration.

Also, consider the recommendations for scores ranging from 21-29 for additional improvement ideas.

Moderate Time Management (Score Range: 21-29)

Manage Information Overload: Set specific times for checking emails and alerts to avoid constant interruptions. Utilize project management tools to streamline work and reduce the cognitive load from juggling too many tasks simultaneously.

Stay Updated but Balanced: Allocate time for learning new technologies relevant to your field, but ensure this is independent of personal time. Continuous learning is crucial but should be balanced with rest and personal activities.

Balance Automation and Personal Touch: Identify tasks that can be automated to save time but also recognize when a personal touch is necessary. You can use automation to support, not replace, your skills.

Promote Open Communication: Encourage open communication within your team or organization. This can lead to more efficient workflows and reduce time wasted on misunderstandings or duplicated efforts.

Employer-Paid Learning: Utilize "windshield time" for personal and professional development through audiobooks or podcasts, especially if your job involves significant travel time. This approach turns otherwise unproductive time into valuable learning opportunities.

Connect Daily To-Dos with Your Goals: Make sure your daily tasks are aligned with your broader goals. This connection ensures that your efforts are directed towards meaningful outcomes, making time management more effective.

Batch Similar Tasks: Group similar tasks together to reduce the cognitive load and increase efficiency. This strategy minimizes the time lost in switching between different types of tasks.

For more information and tools to help you improve your time management skills, stop by our site by scanning the QR below.

Learn more online about this chapter

Chapter 5
Finding Physical and Mental Restoration

In This Chapter

- Benefits of regular exercise for body and mind.

- Integrating exercise sustainably into everyday life.

- Hobbies' role in enhancing productivity and mental sharpness.

- Highlights meditation and mindfulness as tools for emotional stability.

- Presents relaxation techniques as essential for physical and mental well-being.

Chapter 5 strikes a perfect balance, talking directly to skilled trade workers about weaving wellness into the fabric of their daily lives. It's a friendly nudge to remember that life isn't all about work. Those long hours on the job are important, but so is taking time out for some physical activity, diving into hobbies, or sitting quietly to catch a mental break. The chapter offers advice on integrating exercise, leisure, and mindfulness into even the busiest schedules.

It's about prioritizing your health and happiness, with practical tips for finding that sweet spot between professional demands and personal fulfillment. Think of it as your go-to guide for building a more balanced life, where taking care of your body and mind gets as much attention as nailing that next big project.

"I've learned that making a 'living' is not the same thing as 'making a life".

– Maya Angelou, American poet

Learn more online about this chapter

Chapter 5
Finding Physical and Mental Restoration
The importance of regular exercise.

Ah, exercise! For some, it's a love affair; for others, it's a necessary evil; for some, comments like **"who has the time"** ring out.

Unsurprisingly, there is hard evidence that most Americans know exercise is important, yet staying consistent can be tough. Every year, many Americans make New Year's resolutions to get in shape in the coming year, only to fall off the wagon after a month or maybe two. And then there are the marketing folks I hammered on earlier. Like magic, our phones and social media blow up with pitches for diets and now drugs to drop those pounds right around when we are chowing down over this holiday.

Whichever side of the fence you're on, get in shape or not, there's no denying that regular exercise brings myriad benefits for the body and the mind. In today's hectic, always-on digital age, finding ways to achieve physical and mental restoration is not just nice to have – it's probably more essential now than ever.

Let's look at some of the benefits of physical exercise that American pharmaceutical companies would prefer to leave out of add copy ("along with regular exercise") when pitching the latest weight loss drug to us:

The Physical Perks: Let's start with the basics. In its various forms, exercise is a tried and tested way to keep our bodies in shape. And by 'in shape,' I don't just mean looking good in a bathing suit (although that's a bonus!). The physical benefits of regular exercise are extensive, especially when working in skilled trades. Let's face it: your income potential highly depends on your ability to move, lift, and, when needed, contort bodies into natural positions.

A 2019 study published in The Lancet found that people who engaged in regular physical activity had a significantly reduced risk of chronic diseases like heart disease, diabetes, and certain cancers. Not to mention, it's a fantastic way to shed any unwanted pounds and maintain a healthy weight.

As a former skilled trades employer, I will share something rarely said out loud, especially by your employer. If you have obvious general health or mobility issues, YOU WILL miss out on workplace opportunities. If you are okay with office work, this may be okay.

If your heart and soul are to be working with your hands outdoors, get yourself on a sensible workout and diet plan and put in the hard work to make it a sustainable habit. Doing some will reap benefits in your work and personal life.

Chapter 5
Finding Physical and Mental Restoration

The importance of regular exercise.

The Mental Magic: One of the often-overlooked aspects of exercise – the mental benefits. Ever heard of the term "runner's high"? Well, that feel-good sensation isn't exclusive to runners. Aerobic exercises, including jogging, swimming, cycling, walking, gardening, and dancing, have been proven to reduce anxiety and depression.

How does this work? It's all about the chemicals. When we exercise, our brain releases endorphins, those little neurotransmitters that act as natural painkillers. They improve our ability to sleep, which in turn reduces stress. And let's be real, who doesn't need more quality sleep (and less stress)?

Beyond the chemical reactions in our brain, exercise offers a time for introspection, breaking away from the daily grind, and challenging ourselves. Whether beating a personal best in a 10k run or mastering a new yoga pose, these achievements build resilience and boost self-esteem. If you are not a runner, not a fan myself, there are a LOT of Aerobic exercises, in addition to what's mentioned above, that will do the trick. Integrating Exercise Into Your Life.

For the skeptics out there or those who can't find the time, here's the thing: exercise doesn't have to mean spending hours at the gym or running marathons. It's about finding physical activities that you like, ideally love, and integrating them into your life sustainably.

A 2017 report by the American Heart Association recommended a minimum of 150 minutes of moderate exercise or 75 minutes of vigorous exercise per week. That's over 20 minutes a day. A brisk walk, a short home workout, or even dancing around your living room to your favorite tunes – it all counts!

The Bottom Line: Regular exercise emerges as a tool and foundation in our quest for physical and mental restoration. It offers us a way to reconnect with our bodies, challenge our minds, and find moments of clarity in an often chaotic world. So, the next time you feel mentally foggy or physically sluggish, remember that your body and mind might just be craving a good workout. After all, a little sweat can go a long way in paving the path to physical and mental restoration.

Chapter 5
Finding Physical and Mental Restoration
Hobbies and activities outside of work.

Hobbies and Activities Outside of Work:
More so now than ever, striking a balance between work and leisure has never been more essential. It's easy to get wrapped up in the grind of electronic communications on our smartphones, especially late into the night or bringing work home over the weekend. But just like your phone needs a charge after heavy use, our minds and bodies also crave restoration. One of the most effective ways to recharge? Engaging in hobbies and activities outside of work.

The Science Behind Hobbies: The benefits of hobbies aren't just anecdotal. A San Francisco State University study found that employees who engaged in creative hobbies outside of work were more productive and creative in their job roles (Eschleman, K. J., et al., 2014).

These activities, from playing musical instruments to painting, catalyzed relaxation and rejuvenation. And here's the fun part: The improvement wasn't just in job-related tasks. These individuals reported enhanced problem-solving abilities and a more positive outlook towards challenges in their personal lives, too.

Engaging in leisure activities has been associated with a lower risk of dementia, according to the National Institute on Aging. That's right, your weekend gardening sessions or those dance classes are making your brain sharper!

Physical Restoration through Hobbies: Not all hobbies have to be sedentary. From pickleball to salsa dancing, many physically engaging activities tone your muscles and uplift your spirits. It's like nature's own antidepressant. Plus, activities that require focus, like pottery or archery, can be meditative in their own right, pulling you into a "flow" state where time seems to stop, and you're wholly engaged in the moment.

"I am enough of an artist to draw freely upon my imagination. Imagination is more important than knowledge. Knowledge is limited. Imagination encircles the world."

– Albert Einstein, a theoretical physicist, is widely acknowledged as one of the greatest physicists ever.

Chapter 5
Finding Physical and Mental Restoration
Hobbies and activities outside of work.

Mental Rejuvenation and Hobbies: Have you ever noticed how time flies when you're engrossed in some non-work activities or hobbies? That's your brain getting a delightful workout. Activities like reading a novel, working on an old car, or building something in the garage can be amazing distractions from the stresses of day-to-day life.

A study published in the Journal of Positive Psychology (Stavrou, N.A. et al., 2016) found that participants felt more relaxed, happier, and less depressive after engaging in creative activities. So, those DIY projects or cooking experiments aren't just filling your Instagram feed; they're nourishing your mental health!

Balancing Work and Play: It is important to acknowledge that while hobbies can be restorative, striking a balance is crucial. Just like too much work can be draining, overly immersing oneself in hobbies can also become a source of stress, especially if it starts interfering with essential responsibilities. Like many things, too much of anything can be bad, so setting personal limits (or block times) is always smart. A good example of this would be a person who tends to be moderately or extremely competitive. When these folks get into sports, for example, stress brought on by losing a game or match may reduce the mental and even physical benefits of participation. In these cases, selecting a hobby that steers away from competitive situations may be smart when winning at all costs is just who you are.

The Bottom Line: Hobbies and activities outside work provide a vital counterbalance, offering physical and mental restoration. They allow us to tap into parts of ourselves that often remain unexplored during the 9-to-5 routine. So, whether you're strumming a guitar, scaling a mountain, or sketching a sunset, remember, you're not just passing the time—you're investing in your well-being. And if there's one thing research and countless personal anecdotes confirm, this investment always yields positive returns.

> "To sit in the shade on a fine day and look upon verdure is the most perfect refreshment."

– Jane Austen, an English novelist

Chapter 5
Finding Physical and Mental Restoration
The role of meditation, mindfulness, and relaxation techniques.

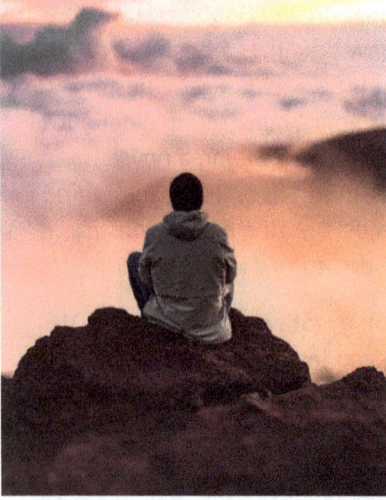

The Power of Meditation: You've probably heard the term 'meditation' thrown around a lot in recent years, maybe in the context of reducing stress or even finding spiritual enlightenment. But what is meditation? At its core, meditation is a practice where an individual uses techniques such as mindfulness or focusing the mind on a particular object, thought, or activity to train attention and awareness and achieve a mentally clear, emotionally calm, and stable state. Sounds fancy, right? Well, the good news is that you don't need to be a monk in the Himalayas to practice it!

According to a Harvard Medical School study from 2011, an eight-week mindfulness-based stress reduction (MBSR) program resulted in demonstrable changes in participants' brain structure. The areas related to learning, memory, and emotion regulation showed increased grey matter density, while the amygdala (associated with stress and anxiety) displayed decreased grey matter density. What does that mean in simple terms? Meditation can genuinely change the way our brains process emotions and reactions!

Let me pause and insert an acknowledgment. Whenever bringing up the subject of meditation and mindfulness to skilled trade professionals, I almost always get a consistent initial response. **How in the (&*$#%^@)** do I work meditation or mindfulness into my life? Followed by, there is just too much to do! My answer to this valid challenge is to take baby steps, not a sprint to the finish. I will cover more on this at the end of this chapter when we check in with Otto and Carol.

The Essence of Mindfulness: As outlined by Jon Kabat-Zinn, the essence of mindfulness is accepting awareness of our current experiences. It's a deliberate practice that encourages us to pause and immerse ourselves in our surroundings, acknowledging each thought, feeling, and sensation without criticism or haste. This approach fosters a deeper connection to the present, enabling individuals to engage more fully with life as it unfolds. Mindfulness teaches us to recognize the passing nature of our thoughts and emotions, offering a pathway to greater peace and resilience in life's inevitable stresses. By anchoring ourselves in the present, we can navigate the complexities of life with greater clarity. This practice doesn't require special equipment or circumstances; it simply requires a commitment to bring our full attention to the present moment.

Chapter 5
Finding Physical and Mental Restoration
The role of meditation, mindfulness, and relaxation techniques.

Unwinding with Relaxation Techniques: Life's hustle and bustle can sometimes leave us feeling physically and mentally drained. That's where relaxation techniques come into play. These techniques, ranging from deep breathing exercises to progressive muscle relaxation, are designed to calm your mind, reduce stress hormones, and promote peace and well-being.!

Research from the Mayo Clinic suggests that relaxation techniques can slow the heart rate, reduce blood pressure, improve digestion, maintain normal blood sugar levels, reduce the activity of stress hormones, increase blood flow to major muscles, and improve concentration. Now, those sound like some benefits we could all use!

There's no one-size-fits-all method here. It's all about finding what works best for you, whether lying down and focusing on your breathing for a few minutes or progressively tensing and then relaxing each muscle group in your body.

The Bottom Line: Meditation, mindfulness, and relaxation techniques offer many benefits proven by science and experienced by countless individuals worldwide. So, carve out a little time for yourself, even a few minutes daily, and dip your toes into these restorative practices. Your body and mind (and likely the people you spend time with at work and home) will thank you for it!

In today's fast-paced world, where technology and deadlines dominate our lives, the importance of self-care cannot be overstated. Meditation and mindfulness exercises can significantly reduce stress, improve concentration, and enhance overall emotional well-being. These practices foster a sense of peace and calm, allowing you to approach life's challenges with a more balanced perspective. Scientific research supports these benefits, showing that regular meditation can lead to changes in the brain associated with decreased anxiety and depression, improved memory, and increased empathy and attention.

"The primary cause of unhappiness is never the situation but your thoughts about it. Be aware of the thoughts you are thinking."

– Eckhart Tolle is a spiritual teacher and writer.

Chapter 5
Finding Physical and Mental Restoration

Otto and Carol's Wellness Journey: Otto and Carol embarked on a transformative wellness journey. They began incorporating regular exercise into their daily routine, recognizing the importance of physical health. They developed new habits and slowly found joy and exhilaration in various activities, including jogging, swimming in the community pool, and playing pickleball with friends on sunny afternoons.

This new regime brought physical benefits, such as improved endurance and strength, mental clarity, and stress relief. They noticed a significant improvement in their sleep patterns and overall well-being. As they delved deeper into their fitness journey, Otto and Carol rediscovered the power and joy of hobbies, especially activities they could do together.

Otto, who had always been fascinated by the intricacies of wood, rekindled his long-forgotten love for woodworking. He spent hours in his garage, meticulously crafting beautiful pieces of furniture, each a testament to his growing skill and creativity.

Carol, on the other hand, found solace and expression in painting. Her canvases became a riot of colors, each stroke reflecting her emotions and thoughts, offering her a creative escape from daily demands.

Initially skeptical, their journey took an unexpected turn when Otto, with Carol's gentle encouragement, began exploring meditation and mindfulness. Together, they learned to appreciate the present moment, finding peace in their daily mindfulness practices. This new practice brought a sense of calm to their hectic lives and enhanced their emotional connection, deepening their understanding and appreciation of each other.

Throughout their journey, Otto and Carol learned valuable lessons about balance, resilience, and the importance of caring for both the mind and the body. They realized that wellness is not just about physical health but encompasses mental, emotional, and spiritual well-being.

Probably the biggest victory of their new lifestyle was that Otto was able to slowly forego his excessive use of alcohol and poor eating habits. This dramatically improved his general health. Even his doctor, who was not easily impressed, was impressed.

1) Prioritize Regular Exercise: Set realistic exercise goals, find enjoyable activities, and consider group classes or activities for motivation. Time investments in this area will keep your doctor off your back and dramatically improve your quality of life.

2) Working out while working: You can get paid to work out because skilled trades can be physically demanding. For example, you are working on the roof of a multi-story building. Instead of roping up your stuff up the side, if the particular building you are working on has standard stairs to the roof, huff your stuff up, taking the stairs. This workload will drive your heart rate the same as you would on a treadmill at the gym, and you will get paid the entire time. Just make sure to be safe about it.

3) Pursue Hobbies and Interests: Encourages dedicating time to hobbies and interests outside of work. This can provide mental relaxation, a sense of achievement, and a way to disconnect from work-related stress.

4) Practice Mindfulness and Meditation: Block time to learn the benefits of mindfulness and meditation, including reducing stress and improving focus and mental clarity. I recommend starting with short sessions and exploring different meditation techniques to find the best.

5) Prioritize Adequate Sleep: Quality sleep for overall health and productivity can't be understated. Do your homework to create a sleep-friendly environment and establish a consistent sleep routine. If you have a TV in your bedroom, consider removing it. Also, consider making your sleeping space an area for rest only by making that space a 100% technology-free zone.

6) Engage in Social Activities: Make time for social interactions to maintain a healthy social life. This can include spending time with family and friends, joining clubs or groups, or participating in community events.

"The resistance that you fight physically in the gym and the resistance that you fight in life can only build a strong character" (linking physical exercise to personal growth)."

-Arnold Schwarzenegger

Chapter 6
Nurturing Relationships Outside of Work

In This Chapter

- Introduction to the emotional bank account concept.

- Warning signs of low emotional account balance.

- Pro tips for avoiding relationship escalation.

- Decoding and applying love languages.

- Investing in Relationships That Matter

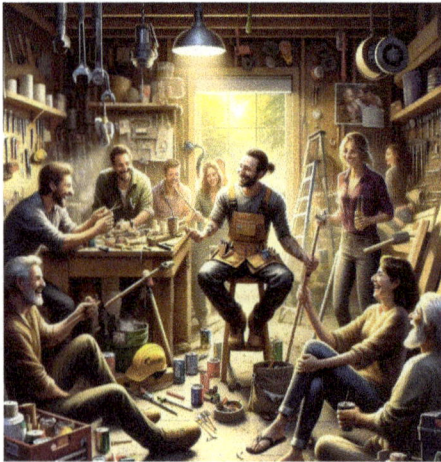

Chapter 6 examines the significance of fostering personal relationships outside the workplace, emphasizing how these connections are pivotal to achieving a well-rounded and fulfilling life. It focuses on the importance of social bonds in enhancing well-being and building a robust support network that can act as a buffer against stress and challenges. The chapter guides skilled trade workers, encouraging them to prioritize their personal lives alongside their careers, promoting balance and happiness.

It underscores the message that while professional success is important, the quality of one's relationships is a key component of overall life satisfaction and resilience.

"In the end, it's not the years in your life that count. It's the life in your years."

- Abraham Lincoln, 16th President of the United States

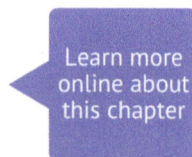

Learn more online about this chapter

Chapter 6
Nurturing Relationships Outside of Work
Investing in relationships that matter

We will open this chapter with another Covey concept, The Emotional Bank Account. Think of it as a bank account of trust and rapport with the people in your life. Every interaction you have, whether with a spouse, friend, family member, or acquaintance, either deposits into or withdraws from this account. Look at some key concepts of the emotional bank account and discover warning signs of a LOW BALANCE. Learning these warning signs, particularly from your significant other, can keep you out of the relationship counselor's chair or, worse, devoirs court.

The Balance: Maintaining a positive balance in our emotional bank accounts requires ongoing effort. A survey by the Pew Research Center found that nearly 58% of people regret not spending enough time with loved ones because of being too caught up with work or other commitments.

When a loved one stops sharing details about their day or expressing their thoughts and feelings, it clearly indicates that the emotional distance is widening. This detachment can stem from a perception that their emotional needs are not being prioritized. Ignoring these signs can significantly strain relationships, fostering resentment and a sense of isolation.

At the opposite end of the spectrum, and even more telling, are offhand comments adults and kids send your way that can be very difficult to interpret. Most of us, especially men, will deflect or ignore these comments.

Some warning signs: Before we get into the details about deposits and withdrawals of the people in your life that are important to you, let's first look at a few warning signs **(See next page)** that, unless you are tuned in, can go right by you. For the sake of brevity, I will focus on comments or actions from a significant other or child that can indicate that your balance is running low in their emotional banking account. When you hear these or something similar, start paying attention because, if you don't, there WILL be trouble heading your way.

PRO TIP: In most cases, what you think is not the problem. Responding to your perception of what you are seeing or hearing with words like "What's your problem?" or "What's going on?" amid the comments or actions on the next page, generally speaking, will result in an escalation. In many cases, disengagement, allowing for tempers to subside a bit, is the smart play. Once tempers have had a chance to subside, come back and ask gentle probing questions to determine the cause of the action or outburst.

Chapter 6
Nurturing Relationships Outside of Work
Investing in relationships that matter

The following tables serve as a guide to understanding behaviors and remarks that signify a depletion in emotional bank accounts, metaphorically representing the amount of trust and goodwill in a relationship. These actions and comments, while varied, share a common theme of indicating a lack of emotional fulfillment or connection, necessitating thoughtful deposits in the form of positive interactions, empathy, and support to restore balance. It's important to recognize that each relationship is unique, and thus, the specific actions or words that deplete one's emotional bank account may differ from person to person.

Warning Comments

Comments From your significant other	Comments From your children
Are you listening to me?	Whatever! Commonly said while not looking away from a screen of some type.
You're never home!	You never listen to me! Commonly followed by a walk away and or door slam.
When are (you or we) going to (task or activity here)?	How come (you or we) don't (enter activity here) anymore?
When your here, your are not really here!	When can (you or we), (enter activity here)? Kids will sometimes insert "you promised" in too.

Unlike "Warning Actions" covered on the next page, comments can be so subtle that they often go unnoticed. Also, unlike actions, these communications may come your way in the non-verbal variety not covered in the above table. These non-verbal communications can happen before or after a verbal comment. In either case, paying attention WILL BE in your best interest.

"Most people do not listen with the intent to understand; they listen with the intent to reply."

- Stephen R. Covey, Author of "The 7 Habits of Highly Effective People".

Nurturing Relationships Outside of Work

Investing in relationships that matter

Warning Actions

Actions By your significant other	Actions By your children
Loss of inter-personal connection	Isolating from you and/or the family.
Reduction in Intimate interactions / sex.	Experimentation with drugs or alcohol
Communication limited to yes, no or small talk.	Sneaking out of the house. Commonly, visiting with others that can be a negative influence.
Bickering over unimportant topics that lead to full blown argements.	Blowing off assigned household chores and/or school homework assignments.

Emotional Bank Account Deposits

Deposits into the emotional bank accounts: Now that you have an idea of the types of comments or actions that tend to accompany a low-emotional bank account, let's jump into a few ways to make meaningful deposits:

1) Understanding the Individual: Everyone is unique. Knowing the other person's likes, dislikes, fears, dreams, and aspirations goes a long way. It's a deposit when we show genuine interest in what is important to others, this fosters a sense of belonging and acceptance and enables us to tailor our interactions to resonate deeply with the individual. By actively listening and engaging with their stories and perspectives, we create a safe space where mutual understanding flourishes, reinforcing the bond through shared empathy and respect.

2) Keeping Commitments: According to research by the American Psychological Association, trust is foundational in relationships. Every time you keep a promise, you're making a deposit. This consistent reliability becomes the cornerstone of a strong relationship, signaling to the other person that they can count on you in both good times and bad.

Chapter 6
Nurturing Relationships Outside of Work
Investing in relationships that matter

3) Clarifying Expectations: Misunderstandings can often arise from misaligned expectations. By clarifying what is expected in a relationship, both parties can operate from a clear standpoint, thereby avoiding potential pitfalls.

4) Show Appreciation: A study published in the Journal of Personality and Social Psychology found that gratitude can lead to better relationships. Regularly expressing **sincere** appreciation can bolster emotional connection and make a deposit.

5) Open Communication: Regular check-ins and open dialogue can prevent small issues from becoming major relationship pitfalls. A quick call between service calls to determine how your significant other's day is going makes a deposit. For the guys, when your spouse comes to you with a problem, you likely don't need to fix it. Many times, the best way to help is **to listen**.

6) Apologize When Necessary: A sincere apology can heal wounds and prevent further deterioration of the emotional bank account. If you screwed up, let them know you are sorry and do your BEST not to repeat.

7) Stay Consistent: Inconsistency in behavior can lead to confusion and mistrust. Being predictable, in a good way, helps maintain a healthy balance in the account.

8) The power of spontaneity: Unexpected expressions of love and caring are among the biggest deposits into the emotional bank account. If your spouse is having a bad day, drive to her work with lunch or a quick picnic at a park nearby. If your kid experiences one of life's many disappointments, like an "F" on an important test or losing a sports tournament, coming home from work early to spend one-on-one time can mean A LOT.

Develop Shared Interests: Participating in activities or hobbies that both partners enjoy can significantly enhance the connection within a relationship. It's about spending time together and creating shared experiences that enrich the bond. Whether taking up a new hobby, exploring new places, or simply engaging in a mutual interest, these shared activities can act as significant deposits into the emotional bank account, fostering a deeper understanding and appreciation for each other.

Practice Empathy: Putting yourself in your partner's shoes and trying to understand their perspective can greatly improve the quality of the relationship. Empathy allows for a more compassionate approach to conflicts and differences, enabling both parties to address issues with sensitivity and awareness.

Chapter 6
Nurturing Relationships Outside of Work
Investing in relationships that matter

Decoding Love Languages: Decoding Love Languages" is an intriguing topic rooted in the ideas presented by Gary Chapman in his 1992 book, "The Five Love Languages." Chapman's concept intertwines beautifully with the emotional bank account theory discussed by Stephen Covey, offering a simple yet profound framework for understanding and nurturing relationships. The core of Chapman's theory lies in the identification and understanding of five distinct love languages:

1) Words of Affirmation: This love language involves expressing affection through spoken affection, praise, or appreciation. It's important to realize that what counts as a meaningful affirmation can vary greatly from person to person.

2) Quality Time: This language is about giving the other person your undivided attention. It's not just about being in the same room but about focusing on your partner and making the most of your time together.

3) Receiving Gifts: For some people, what makes them feel most loved is to receive a gift. This doesn't necessarily mean expensive or elaborate presents; it's more about the thought and effort behind the gift.

4) Acts of Service: Anything you do to ease the burden of responsibilities weighing on an 'Acts of Service' person will speak volumes. It could be as simple as cooking a meal, doing the laundry, or running errands.

5) Physical Touch: This language concerns more than just the bedroom. A person whose primary language is physical touch is, not surprisingly, very touchy. Hugs, pat on the back, and thoughtful touches can all be ways to show excitement, concern, care, and love.

The key takeaway from Chapman's theory is the understanding that everyone expresses and receives love differently. What resonates deeply with one person might hold a different significance for another. Therefore, understanding and acknowledging these differences is crucial for the health and longevity of relationships.

Open and honest communication with your partner or loved ones is essential to discover their unique love languages. This understanding allows for a more tailored approach to expressing love and affection.

Chapter 6
Nurturing Relationships Outside of Work
The importance of social connections.

Fostering relationships outside our jobs is not just about having fun; it's also vital for our well-being, creativity, and happiness.

Why Social Connections Matter: Researchers have been studying social connections for years, and the consensus is clear: humans are social animals. According to a study published in Psychological Bulletin, strong social connections can lead to a whopping 50% increased chance of longevity. That's right! Having close friends and family can add years to your life.

Beyond the obvious health benefits, there's also the aspect of emotional well-being. A study from the University of Texas highlighted that social interactions can help reduce feelings of depression, anxiety, and other mental health issues. When we connect with others, our brain releases oxytocin—the "love hormone." This makes us feel good and acts as a buffer against stress, which, let's face it, we all have plenty of.

The Creativity Link: If you're thinking, "Well, I'm not much of a social butterfly, and I'm doing just fine," consider this: social connections have been found to boost creativity. Interacting with a diverse group of people outside your immediate work circle can expose you to new ideas, perspectives, and inspirations. Remember that groundbreaking idea or sudden inspiration you got while chatting with a friend at a coffee shop or during a family dinner? That's the magic of diverse social interactions.

Finding the Balance: Like everything in life, it's about balance. You don't need to be the life of the party or have a jam-packed social calendar to reap the benefits of social connections. Simply making time for a weekly coffee catch-up with a friend or regular family dinners can make a difference.

The Longevity Factor: Research suggests that mental health can be pivotal in longevity. A study published in "Psychosomatic Medicine" found a strong correlation between social relationships and lifespan. Individuals with robust social ties were observed to have a significantly lower risk of premature death compared to those with weaker social bonds. This connection is believed to stem from the support system provided by strong social networks, which can help individuals navigate through stress, encourage healthier lifestyle choices, and provide a sense of belonging and purpose. Thus, investing in your social connections isn't just about improving your current quality of life; it could be extending it.

Chapter 6
Nurturing Relationships Outside of Work
The importance of social connections.

Digital vs. Real-Life Connections: Referring to the Where'swhere's Waldo example earlier in this book, equating our online connections with real-life interactions is tempting. The convenience and reach of digital communication are undeniable, but as Stanford University research highlights, face-to-face interactions hold a unique emotional depth and foster stronger bonds. While digital tools like tweets and emoji-laden messages have their place, they can only partially replicate the nuances and richness of in-person conversations.

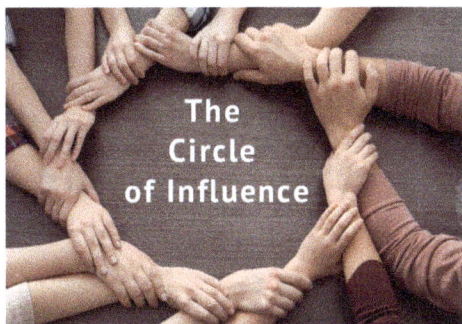

The Circle of Influence

Consider the concept called the "Circle of Influence" (COI). This framework becomes particularly relevant when examining the generational shifts in communication and socialization, especially for those who've grown up with pervasive Internet access and social media - notably Generation Z, born between 1997 and 2012.

This demographic, despite possessing an unprecedentedly vast COI, has experienced high rates of depression. The paradox lies in their social connections: expansive yet lacking depth. This phenomenon raises critical questions about the quality and authenticity of digital interactions.

To contextualize, let's look at previous generations. The Baby Boomers (born 1955 to 1964), Generation X (born 1965 to 1980), and Millennials (born 1981 to 1996) witnessed a gradual integration of technology into daily life. During the "Boomer Times," human interactions were predominantly face-to-face, fostering genuine interpersonal relationships and close-knit COIs. These relationships were characterized by a deeper sense of care and mutual understanding, qualities less frequently found in today's more transient and surface-level connections.

With Generation Z, the advent of advanced technology blurred the lines between true friendships and casual acquaintances, as previously covered. Particularly in affluent regions like America, the COI saw exponential growth. However, this expansion came at a cost. Most social connections morphed into more akin to acquaintances rather than real friendships.

This shift highlights the critical need for balance. While digital connections serve a purpose, they should maintain the value of real-life, emotionally resonant interactions. The challenge for current and future generations is to navigate this landscape, cherishing the convenience of digital connections while actively seeking and valuing the irreplaceable depth of face-to-face relationships.

Chapter 6
Nurturing Relationships Outside of Work

The importance of social connections.

Here are a few studies that support some of the negative impacts of technology on GenZ.

Research indicates that technology has negatively impacted Generation Z (those born from the mid-1990s to the early 2010s), particularly through social media.

Here are some key findings from different sources:

1) A study highlighted by **McKinsey & Company** found that Gen Z respondents from Europe and Oceania were most likely to report negative impacts from social media, with a significant number perceiving a detrimental effect on their mental health.

2) **Psychology Today** reports that compulsive social media use is widespread among teenagers and college students, which is recognized to be harmful to their mental health. Heavy social media usage has been connected to increased rates of anxiety and depression among Gen Z individuals.

3) The same **McKinsey** survey also pointed out that female Gen Zers, in particular, experience negative effects from social media use, which are often related to body image and self-esteem issues.

4) A study cited by **Limely** discusses how the attachment to technology during early development can disrupt an individual's ability to process information, regulate emotions, and focus on tasks. This attachment also fosters a need for instant gratification, which is prevalent among Millennials and Gen Z due to the interconnected nature of today's society.

5) **Medical News Today** lists several psychological, social, and health-related negative effects of technology, such as reduced creativity, delays in language and social-emotional development, physical inactivity leading to obesity, poor sleep quality, and social issues, including incompatibility and isolation

Bottom Line: Nurturing real relationships outside work is more than a feel-good activity. It's an investment in your well-being, creativity, and overall happiness. So, the next time you consider skipping that friend's gathering or family event for work, remember the benefits of social connections and make time for it. After all, we're hardwired for it!

Chapter 6
Nurturing Relationships Outside of Work
Building and maintaining a support system.

The timeless proverb, "No man is an island," encapsulates the profound impact of our personal lives on our overall well-being and happiness. This truth holds even for those deeply immersed in their work. Despite the allure of career achievements, the value of cultivating relationships outside the office is undeniable and substantial.

This importance is not just anecdotal; it's backed by scientific research. A 2017 study in the journal Personal Relationships revealed a remarkable finding: strong social connections can increase the likelihood of longevity by 50%. This statistic is a testament to the potential life-extending benefits of our relationships.

Why Nurturing Social Connections is Essential

1) Enhancement of Mental Health: The role of a robust support network in mental health cannot be overstated. Research from the University of North Carolina at Chapel Hill underscores this, showing that individuals with close social ties exhibit lower levels of stress hormones. This finding suggests that our social gatherings – from casual brunches with friends to engaging book clubs – are more than just enjoyable pastimes; they serve as vital defenses against stress. In moments of challenge, whether personal or professional, the availability of a trusted friend or family member for support and advice is invaluable. These relationships act as a safety net, providing comfort and stability during times of potential turmoil.

2) Quality Trump's Quantity: Interestingly, the significance of social connections isn't in their number but in their depth. Research from the American Sociological Review points out that a few intimate friendships contribute more to our happiness than a wide circle of acquaintances. This insight suggests a shift in focus; instead of diluting efforts across numerous superficial relationships, it is more beneficial to cultivate deeper connections with a select few.

Our well-being, mental health, and even longevity are intricately linked to the quality of our social connections. These relationships offer a sanctuary from stress, a source of happiness, and a critical component of a fulfilling life. Therefore, the emphasis should be on nurturing these connections and recognizing their profound impact on our lives.

Chapter 6
Nurturing Relationships Outside of Work

Otto and Carol - Work on their Emotional Bank Account: Like many couples do, dealing with the everyday realities of maintaining a healthy emotional balance amidst the pressures of life. After learning about the emotional bank account concept at a couples workshop recommended by their marriage counselor, they both started reflecting on how every interaction strengthens or strains their bond.

Otto recalled recent misunderstandings that led to withdrawals from their emotional bank account. On the other hand, Carol feels the strain of these withdrawals, sensing a growing distance between them.

With their new knowledge, they start recognizing the warning signs of a low balance in their relationship. Otto sees how his preoccupation with work and lack of attention has depleted Carol's account.

Carol, feeling neglected, expresses her concerns, mirroring the patterns described in their newfound knowledge. This open communication becomes their first significant deposit into their emotional accounts. They begin to understand the uniqueness of their needs and the importance of keeping commitments.

Together, they embark on making meaningful deposits into their emotional account. Otto starts by planning a surprise weekend getaway, focusing on quality time and heartfelt conversations. Carol, embracing the concept of words of affirmation, leaves Otto with heartfelt notes and messages, acknowledging his efforts and expressing her appreciation.

As Otto and Carol navigate these changes, they also confront their twin boys' challenges in the digital age. After a while together, they started to understand the boys' warning signs and found creative ways to make deposits in their accounts.

"Husbands and wives, first be faithful to each other. Second, keep the romance going all of your life by courting each other every day."

- Zig Ziglar, American author, salesman, and motivational speaker

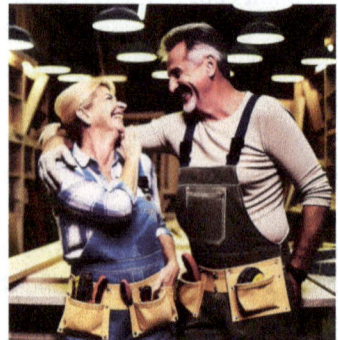

Nurturing Relationships Outside of Work

1) Investing in Important Relationships: Plan regular, undistracted time with loved ones, highlighting the psychological benefits of deep, meaningful connections for stress relief and overall well-being.

2) Building Strong Social Connections: Consider joining special interest groups or volunteering to expand your social circles. These activities can lead to new perspectives and reduce feelings of isolation.

3) Maintaining a Support System: Block out time in your time management application to build a diverse support network, including professional guidance when necessary, to navigate life's challenges more effectively.

4) Balancing Work and Personal Life: Create 'no work' zones at home or schedule 'off-the-grid' time to disconnect from work and engage with family and friends.

5) Communication and Quality Time: Learn techniques for building open communication and shared experiences in your personal relationship that foster understanding and closeness.

6) Investing in Personal Growth: Learn new ways to advocate for continuous learning and self-improvement. This could involve taking up new hobbies, enrolling in educational courses, or attending workshops and seminars. Highlight how personal development can lead to increased self-esteem and a deeper understanding of one's abilities and potential.

"Work is a rubber ball. If you drop it, it will bounce back. The other four balls – family, health, friends, integrity – are made of glass. If you drop one of these, it will be irrevocably scuffed, nicked, perhaps even shattered"

-Gary W. Keller, Executive Chairman of Keller Williams. Keller Williams is recognized as the largest real estate company in the world

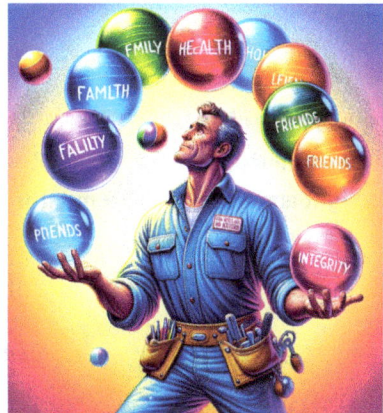

Chapter 7
The role of faith in maintaining balance in your life.

In This Chapter

- Exploring the anchoring effect of faith in turbulent times

- Faith's role in community building and support

- How faith offers perspective during life's challenges

- The benefits of faith-based emotional regulation practices

- Faith-inspiring, purpose-driven action in daily life.

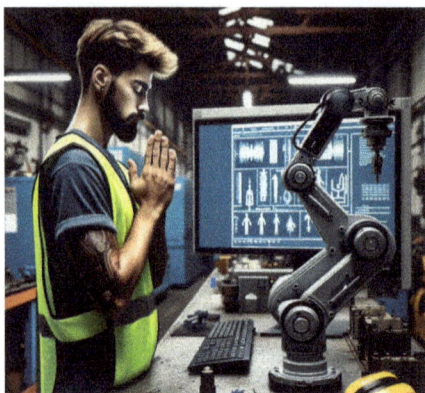

Chapter 7 delves into the profound role of faith in achieving balance in life, especially for skilled trade workers confronting unique challenges. It articulates why faith is beneficial and essential in navigating the complexities of maintaining equilibrium amidst the demands of their profession. This chapter underscores faith as a cornerstone for discerning purpose, providing a source of strength, resilience, and guidance.

Engaging narratives and insightful discussionsillustrate how faith acts as an anchor, helping individuals weather the storms of life while fostering a sense of community and belonging. This exploration into the interplay between faith and balance offers readers a compelling argument for integrating spiritual practices in their quest for a harmonious life.

"Faith is the strength by which a shattered world shall emerge into the light."

– Helen Keller

An American author, political activist, and lecturer. Miss Keller lost both her sight and hearing at 19 months of age.

Learn more online about this chapter

Chapter 7
The role of faith in maintaining balance in your life.
Why faith is essential in navigating these challenges and ensuring balance.

You've probably spotted 'Faith is essential' in the subtitle above and thought, 'Okay, what's this all about?' I get it. Faith these days can get folks a little squirmy. In some circles, faith can be considered a trigger word. But could you stick with me? You may end up feeling unexpectedly curious. Let's unpack this together.

A personal story about faith: As you have progressed through this book, we have been checking in on the characters Otto and Carol. Early in their story, you learn that Otto has Dyslexia. Well, that's me. So, reading the Bible was a no-go. Borrowing a popular phrase, the Bible in written form is WORD SALAD to my brain. Thank you, God, for the miracle of listening to the Bible on audio.

In my earlier years, my parents only went to a church for weddings and funerals. On the other hand, my Grandmother insisted that I join her every few weeks at one of the MANY churches she attended throughout my childhood. These churches were off the hook, even to me now. This was fire and brimstone, shaking uncontrollably and speaking in tongues, that type of off-the-hook. NUTS! The trifecta of my parents not being church folks, not being able to read the Bible functionally, and my early experiences attending church with my Grandmother, I came to the conclusion that organized religion was not for me.

Flash forward to my late teens and early twenties; I, on my own, attended church occasionally when invited by some friends, eventually joining a youth-adult group. Looking back, being honest here, it was more about meeting the girls than the Lord; just saying :-) Good thing God's patient.

My crash course in prayer and God's power: Like most kids my age, I loved to play baseball. One day, I played a game called Hot Box (or Pickle) with some classmates. Basically, you run your butt off between two bases and try not to get tagged out. During a heated pickle, I turned my head to look at the kid throwing the ball, and my right eye was struck hard by the ball. Almost immediately, my eyesight in that eye started to get cloudy, effectively scaring the crap out of me.

The doctor told my parents and me that the impact had caused blood vessel bleeding in the back of my eye that would likely result in losing my eye. They recommended that I patch both of my eyes for a week to see if the vessel stopped bleeding and, if it did, the eye would probably survive, and the clarity of my sight should return to normal in a few weeks. If not, I would end up with a glass eye.

The role of faith in maintaining balance in your life.

Why faith is essential in navigating these challenges and ensuring balance.

So there I was, lying around for a week, TOTALLY blind. It took me a few days to get past the freakout stage. After that, I decided to start praying, baby! At first, it felt VERY uncomfortable.

After a few days of praying during my days of blindness, I started to feel something. I started to get these feelings, and even some dreams, that everything would be okay.

Then came the doctor's visit day. I went into the appointment at peace; at the time, I didn't know if I would see with both eyes again. Then bandages came off.

When the doctor removed my left eye patch, so far, so good. Things were moving in slow motion. The right patch slowly got pulled away, and it was up to me to open that eyelid.

When I did, I was amazed; I COULD SEE PERFECTLY. The doctor said how cloudy my sight was. I said it was like the accident never happened. In disbelief, he dilated my eye and took a look at the area at the back of my eye that was hemorrhaging blood into my eye only seven days prior. "I can't believe it," he said. He reported that he could barely see any trace of injury. He showed my Mom and me pictures of before and after, and we could not believe it.

From that day forward, I became a believer in God and prayer works; however, many years later, I developed enough curiosity about faith in Jesus to invest in that relationship. Despite being a late bloomer, my family and I have been (and continue to be) blessed in more ways than I can count.

The basis of this story is to be curious and consider turning to prayer when faced with life challenges.

How's life in your bubble?: I had an interesting conversation with my youngest son, David. While driving to play pickleball one night, he said he felt like he was running up against the boundaries of his bubble. Seeing that it is rare these days for twenty-something, especially young men, to express their feelings, I quickly tuned in and asked what he meant. The gist of David's comment was coming across feelings of isolation and disconnect. Call if it's a coincidence or messaging from a higher power; I was working on this very chapter at the time of this conversation. When I returned to the office the next day, I looked into David's comment and was surprised at what I found.

Chapter 7
The role of faith in maintaining balance in your life.
Why faith is essential in navigating these challenges and ensuring balance.

David's enlightening comment about the bubble and feelings of dissolution and disconnection are valid. Since I have heard similar comments on the podcast from other skilled trade pros, like my son, I decided to examine why Gen Y and Z are experiencing higher rates of isolation or loneliness than prior generations. I also wanted to examine how Gen Y and Z feel about faith today.

This graphic supports where David came from that night on his way to play pickleball. As surveys go, this was a large sample with a simple message. Gen Y (folks David's age) and Gen Z are indeed struggle with feeling lonely.

Gen Z Is Lonely
Percent of U.S. adults who are lonely, shown as demographics

61% of all U.S. adults reported feeling lonely, which is up 7% from last year

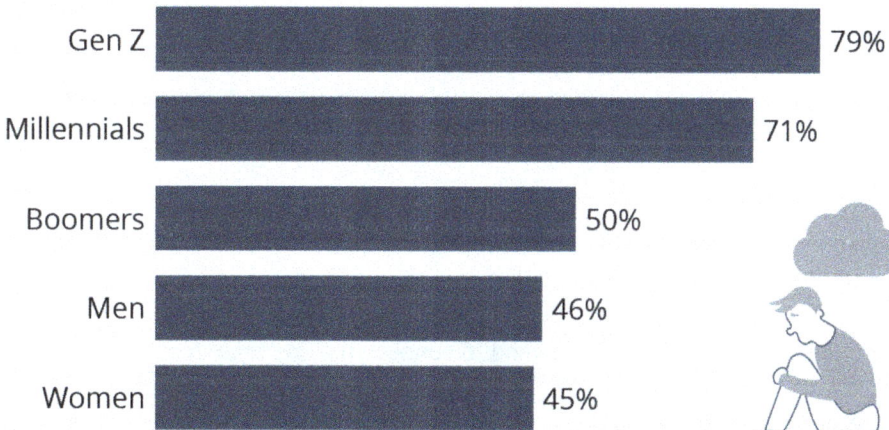

Demographic	Percent
Gen Z	79%
Millennials	71%
Boomers	50%
Men	46%
Women	45%

n=10,441 adults
Survey was conducted during the summer of 2019
Source: Ipsos Polling for Cigna U.S. Loneliness Index

So, why are younger Americans isolated and or lonely? On the next page, you will find some interesting findings supported by a growing body of evidence.

Once we can understand more about what is going on with the two generations that will make up the majority of workers in America in the next few years, I will propose how faith can play a role in addressing concern trends towards feelings of isolation, loneliness, and depression.

Chapter 7
The role of faith in maintaining balance in your life.
Why faith is essential in navigating these challenges and ensuring balance.

90

The following data was gleaned from an article in Psychology Today. To see this article in its entirety, scan the QR below.

1) Overstimulation: Preoccupation has skyrocketed in recent years. We are all distracted. We are distracted by work, house chores, progress, underline social media, the activities of today, the commitments of tomorrow, and then relieving the stress from it all. Our distractions are eating up most of our cognitive resources, leaving little to nothing for focusing on others.

We'd all like to think we wouldn't turn our back on humanity, yet that is what we do every day when we choose an impersonal email over empathy, TikTok over tactile, a text over touch, or Instagram over in-person.

We live in a world today where it takes little effort to fill your time. An endless amount of content in the palm of our hands has allowed us to consume news and entertainment whenever and wherever we are. We've become a culture more focused on strengthening our Wi-Fi connections than strengthening our interpersonal connections. We need to trade our connectable technology for a more connectable team. Is it overstimulation that causes loneliness, or is Gen Z overstimulated to distract from the pain of their loneliness? Either way, overstimulation leaves Gen Z less time to connect, making them feel lonelier.

2) Social Media: Beating up on social media a bit more, studies show that very heavy social media users are significantly more likely to feel alone, isolated, left out, and without companionship. Social media has caused a comparison trap. Comparing our life to someone else's highlight reel leads to questions like, am I good enough, smart enough, wealthy enough, etc.?

According to Roger Patulny, associate professor of sociology at the University of Wollongong in Australia, while heavy social media users experience more loneliness, evidence suggests social media use decreases loneliness among highly social people. Why the contradiction? "Social media is most effective in tackling loneliness when used to enhance existing relationships or forge new meaningful connections...>

The role of faith in maintaining balance in your life.
Why faith is essential in navigating these challenges and ensuring balance.

...> On the other hand, it is counterproductive if used as a substitute for real-life social interaction. Thus, it is not social media itself, but how we integrate it into our lives that impacts loneliness," says Patulny.

The online social connections available are astounding and promising, and they are a great start to boosting belonging for some. But the quantity of connections doesn't make up for the quality of connections needed to lessen loneliness. High-quality connections online are **rare** because of how status-driven and polished the environments tend to be.

3. Dependency Shift: Information is no longer centralized in a family member, neighbor, coworker, or leader. Information is decentralized, empowering humanity to seek knowledge (or help) individually. Humans are naturally dependent on each other. However, we once were more dependent.

In the past, if your faucet was leaking in your home, you may have knocked on your neighbor's door to ask for a plumber's recommendation. Or you may have called a family member or friend to have them guide you through the process to fix it. Today, your first step would likely be to open YouTube and search for "how to fix a leaky faucet."

The same is true at work. In the past, if you didn't know how to create a pivot table in Excel, you would walk around to your coworkers' desks to ask who knew how to do such Excel wizardry. Today, a simple YouTube search yields a 2:14-minute video outlining what to do. During the writing, applications like CHAT-GPT leverage A.I. to write Excel formulas. Just copy and paste, and you're done.

Gen Y and Z aren't the only parties guilty of leveraging Google or YouTube to gain knowledge. Like mussel memory, many of us are now quick to turn to the supercomputers in our pockets before we "inconvenience" someone else. This is okay; this is useful and expeditious. But if these subtle non-human-reliant actions are commonplace, we must build more time for meaningful face-to-face, human-to-human connections elsewhere. Without those connections, it is only a matter of time before the most interfering self-starters begin to feel isolated and depressed.

As our dependency shifts more and more to technology, automation, and artificial intelligence—without a counterbalance—our loneliness will grow.

Chapter 7
The role of faith in maintaining balance in your life.
Why faith is essential in navigating these challenges and ensuring balance.

This next graphic from a 2020 study shows that there has been a consistent increase in non-affiliation to religion, particularly within the Gen Y (millennial) and Gen Z demographics.

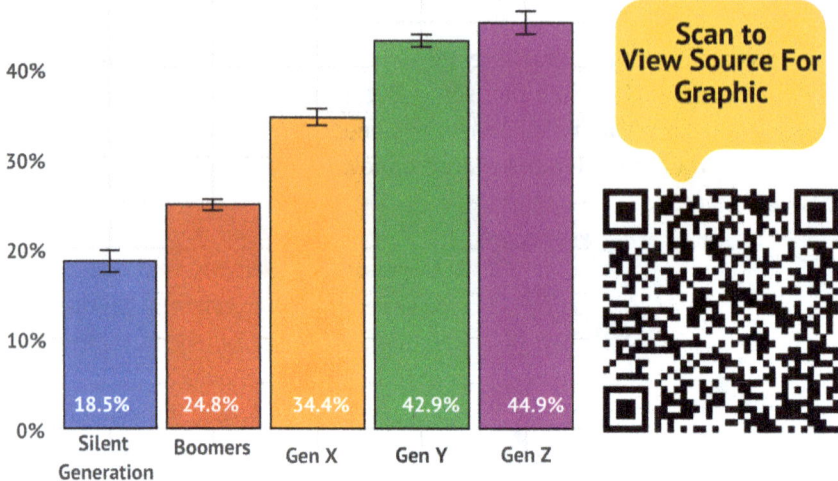

Scan to View Source For Graphic

@ryanburge

Is there a connection between these two studies? At the very least, it would support a healthy curiosity about faith and its potential path to a happier, more fulfilled life.

With that food for thought out of the way, let's look at the role faith can play in the life of a skilled trade pro. Why is this subject especially relevant to skilled trade pros? Answer: unlike white-collar jobs, it is common for skilled trades workers to be physically isolated from other humans. Long drives from job site to job site, a plumber running pipe on a roof, or a utility worker out in a bucket truck trying to get the power back on are just a few examples.

Input from a former Athiest: If you are curious about faith and how it can affect your daily life, I would like to introduce you to an excellent book that was very helpful to me and millions of others who wish to address the question of faith.

Lee Strobel's book titled "The Case For Christ" gives readers a front-row seat at how an atheist with an incredible investigative mind initially set out to disprove the Bible and became a believer in Christ.

Strobel was a crime reporter for a major newspaper who applied his award-winning investigative chops to Christianity, the Bible, and the story of Jesus. As an atheist, he spent much time trying to punch holes in Jesus's life, death, and resurrection. His book became a huge best seller, published in many languages, and eventually made it to the big screen, becoming a hit movie by the same title. I encourage you to check the Case for The Case For Christ book, movie, or audiobook.

Chapter 7
The role of faith in maintaining balance in your life.
Why faith is essential in navigating these challenges and ensuring balance.

Let's face it, the world is filled with obstacles, heartbreaks, and uncertainties. Life can often feel like a juggling act, and just when you think you've got a handle on it, something else comes hurtling your way. During these times, faith can provide you with the extra persistence or grit to make it through difficult situations that make their way into everyone's life. Here are some key aspects about faith and how it can help you:.

1) Anchoring Effect of Faith: First and foremost, faith provides an anchoring effect. Life's unpredictable waves can toss us around, leaving us unsettled and adrift. Faith acts as a grounding force. It offers a sense of purpose and meaning, vital when navigating the rough waters of life. A study from the Harvard T.H. Chan School of Public Health showed that individuals with high levels of religious participation had a lower risk of depression and felt more optimistic about their futures. The feeling of belonging and being part of something bigger provides a solid foundation to build resilience and face adversities.

2) Community and Support System: When discussing belonging, considering the community of faith is worth some consideration. Whether it's a church, prayer group, or gathering like-minded individuals, faith has a knack for bringing people together. And there's undeniable power in that. A 2018 study published in Social Psychological and Personality Science pointed out that social connections, often cultivated within faith communities, can enhance psychological well-being, reducing loneliness and increasing feelings of self-worth.

3) A Framework for Perspective: Life's challenges are often a matter of perspective. While it's essential to acknowledge pain and sorrow, faith provides a framework to view them as temporary and surmountable. Many religious texts and spiritual teachings emphasize the transient nature of human suffering and the idea that, with patience and perseverance, brighter days are on the horizon.

4) Emotional Regulation and Coping: Beyond perspective, faith offers tools for emotional regulation. Many faith practices, such as prayer or meditation, can help soothe the nervous system. In 2013, JAMA Psychiatry published a study indicating that meditation, a component of many faiths, could reduce symptoms of anxiety, depression, and pain. These faith-based rituals, especially prayer, can be powerful coping mechanisms when practiced consistently.

Chapter 7
The role of faith in maintaining balance in your life.
Why faith is essential in navigating these challenges and ensuring balance.

5) Purpose-Driven Action: The powerful motivator to lead lives infused with intention and purpose is at the heart of many spiritual beliefs. Connecting with a cause greater than ourselves naturally propels us towards actions that resonate with our deepest values and principles. This push towards purposeful engagement—whether through acts of charity, community involvement, or everyday kindness—serves as a dynamic counterweight to life's adversities, empowering us to be agents of positive change.

The significance of faith, whether tied to a specific religion or a broader spiritual awareness, in fostering a balanced life is undeniable. It acts as a steadfast anchor, offers a nurturing community, broadens our perspective, equips us with emotional coping strategies, and inspires purposeful action. Challenges are an inevitable part of life, yet with faith as our compass, we can navigate these with poise and equilibrium. So, when the world feels heavy and you're searching for light, remember the transformative power of faith—a force that can propel you forward, no matter the hurdles.

Below is an interesting study of over 10,000 Americans between the ages of 18 and 45 conducted in 2019. They asked participants to rate their level of importance in dealing with some of the most common challenges in life.

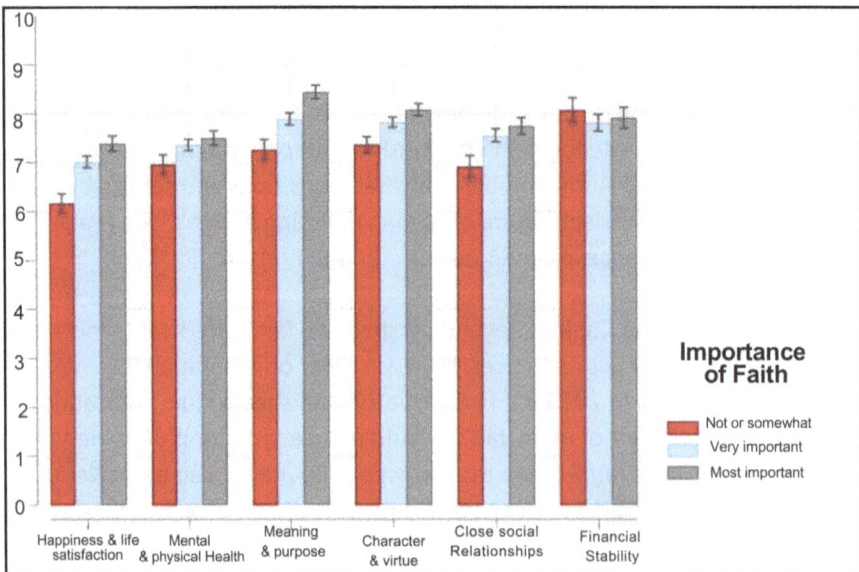

Harvard Flourishing Domains by the Importance of Religion / Faith

Chapter 7
The role of faith in maintaining balance in your life.
The unique challenges faced by those in skilled trades concerning faith.

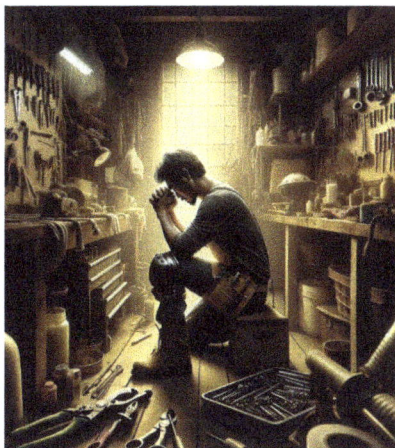

As mentioned, skilled trades encompass many professions—from carpenters and electricians to plumbers and welders. Often, these individuals work in environments that demand precision, attention to detail, and much physical effort. Quiet spaces, Safe spaces, and puppy petting rooms that you see on college campuses and even some large companies are not on the schedule for our skilled trade heroes. The hours can be long, and the tasks can sometimes be dangerous. It's within these pressures and demands that the role of faith manifests in unique ways.

One of the primary challenges skilled tradespeople face is the physical toll their work can take on their bodies. A research study published in the "Journal of Occupational Rehabilitation" highlighted how chronic musculoskeletal pain is prevalent among those in manual labor professions. In this context, faith often plays a dual role: a source of strength and perseverance during tough times and a well of gratitude for the good days.

Another challenge is the unpredictability of work. Many tradespeople work on a contractual basis. When one project ends, there might be another lined up later. These fluctuations can lead to financial and emotional stress. When these situations pop up, faith offers hope. A belief that things will work out, even when the immediate future seems uncertain. An article from "Forbes" in 2019 discussed how faith or spirituality can be a strong anchor in financial uncertainty, grounding individuals and helping them navigate the ups and downs with a clearer mind.

It's essential to note that faith isn't just about dealing with challenges. For many skilled tradespeople, their work is an act of passion—a craft. Creating, repairing, or building can be seen as a spiritual experience. Each project can be a testament to their faith, whether in their abilities, the materials they work with, or a higher power they believe guides their hands.

In social contexts, skilled trades can sometimes be overlooked or undervalued compared to professions that require a university degree. The pride in one's craft and the tangible results of hard work are where faith intertwines with self-worth. Believing in the value of one's work, even in the face of societal pressures, requires a deep-seated faith in oneself and one's trade.

Chapter 7
The role of faith in maintaining balance in your life.

The unique challenges faced by those in skilled trades concerning faith.

For many working in skilled trades, faith isn't just an abstract concept—it's an integral part of daily life. Whether it's finding the strength to push through physical pain, the hope in uncertain times, or the pride in one's craft, faith is a guiding light. Recognizing and understanding this relationship can help us appreciate the profound depth and resilience of those working with their hands and hearts daily.

Otto and Carol - Otto and Carol's connection through faith, though subtle, became a source of hope and resilience in their respective fields. With his hands shaped by the rigors of construction, Otto found solace and purpose in every nail he drove and the wall he erected. His craft was more than just building structures; it manifested his faith - a belief in creating something lasting and meaningful from the mundane.

He approached each project not just as a job to be done but as an opportunity to infuse his work with the values he held dear.

On the other hand, Carol (after returning to work) navigated the high-pressure world of corporate strategy with the poise and grace that set her apart. Her faith was her anchor, enabling her to stay grounded amidst the chaos of tight deadlines and high-stakes decisions. She didn't just lead her team; she inspired them, fostering an environment where every member felt valued and empowered. Carol's approach to leadership was steeped in her belief that every challenge was an opportunity to grow and learn, a chance to demonstrate the strength and resilience born of faith.

Though personal and unobtrusive, their faith became a silent force that shaped their approach to work and life. It was in the quiet moments of reflection, in the deliberate choices they made, and in the way they interacted with those around them that their faith shone brightest. Otto and Carol's story is not just about the convergence of two distinctly different professional paths but about how faith can be a guiding light, offering direction and purpose in the most unexpected ways.

Their journey together, intertwined by their shared beliefs, serves as a powerful narrative of how faith can transcend the confines of personal belief and become a transformative force in the professional realm. The story highlights the importance of staying true to one's values and beliefs, no matter the setting.

The role of faith in maintaining balance in your life.

1) Be curious about faith: If the stories I have shared in this chapter, or perhaps some unexplained events (good and not so good) that have occurred in your life, have left you wondering, an exploration into faith and the power of prayer may lead to some answers for you. It couldn't hurt, right?

2) Be curious about faith: If the stories I have shared in this chapter, or perhaps some unexplained events (good and not so good) that have occurred in your life, have left you wondering, an exploration into faith and the power of prayer may lead to some answers for you. It couldn't hurt, right?

3) Understanding Faith's Role: Emphasizes reflecting on how faith shapes perspectives and coping mechanisms. Suggests dedicating time to spiritual activities or practices that reinforce faith.

4) Faith in the Context of Skilled Trades: Encourages tradespeople to explore how their faith aligns with their work ethics and values and how it can provide resilience in challenging work environments.

5) Integrating Faith into Daily Life: Recommends creating a daily routine that includes faith-based practices, such as prayer or meditation, to foster a sense of peace and purpose.

6) Seeking Community Support: Advises joining faith-based groups or communities for additional support, shared experiences, and a sense of belonging.

7) Faith as a Tool for Reflection and Growth: Suggests using faith as a foundation for self-reflection, to evaluate life choices and priorities, and to seek personal growth and understanding.

"Through hard work, perseverance and a faith in God, you can live your dreams."

-Dr. Ben Carson, renowned neurosurgeon, author, and politician

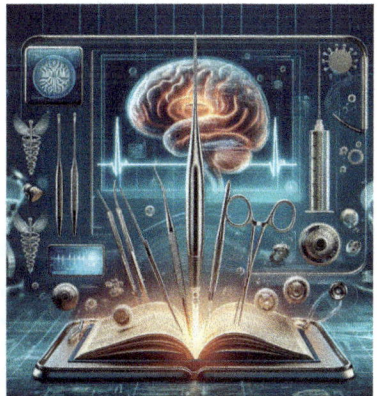

In This Chapter

- Continual Learning is Essential.

- Mentorship's Power.

- Microlearning Efficiency.

- Hands-on Learning Benefits

- Managing Stress and Mindfulness.

Chapter 8 focuses on navigating skills development challenges for skilled trade workers, aiming to prevent the overwhelming effects of continuous learning. It delves into strategies for balancing job demands with growth opportunities and highlights the importance of leveraging technology to make learning more efficient. This chapter guides professionals in skilled trades to pursue their development without succumbing to burnout.

"The only way to do great work is to love what you do. If you haven't found it yet, keep looking. Don't settle."

- Steve Jobs, Co-founder, Apple Computer

Learn more online about this chapter

Skills Development Without Getting Overwhelmed
Continued learning without burning out.

Continued learning is essential to being at the top of your game. Most people who are serious about their careers know this. Like many worthwhile things, like career, marriage, and parenting, constantly improving requires consistent effort.

Can you have a bad day? YES. Are you going to get things right every time? NO. The trick is maintaining a consistent improvement effort in professional and personal development. The challenge with making a consistent effort is that life, which I am sure you have realized by now, tends to be very dynamic. Distractions are constant, and maintaining a consistent effort, especially during hard times, can be VERY difficult. Sprinkle in the work-life balance challenges; it can be easy to get burnt out, and soon, before you know it, you have replaced the continued learning habit that helps you in important areas of your life with habits that can hurt you.

Here are a few tips that can help keep the flame of learning alive. I urge you to consider the following:

1) Getting Mentors on your team: A crucial yet often neglected factor in achieving success in skilled trades is the capability to identify, recruit, and actively engage with both personal and professional mentors. This approach is not just about learning skills but about understanding the nuances of the trade through experienced eyes. Consider the profound impact of forming relationships with individuals who have navigated the same path you're on and encountered numerous challenges along the way.

These mentors can provide invaluable insights, helping you sidestep common pitfalls, thereby saving you months or even years of trial and error. This mentorship can significantly accelerate your career progression and personal growth, surpassing the pace you might achieve solo.

You might question why seasoned professionals would be inclined to mentor someone like you. **Here's an insight:** As people advance in their careers and lives, many develop a genuine desire to impart their wisdom and experiences to others. This tendency is more widespread than you might assume. Accessing these individuals' deep wells of knowledge can be a formidable advantage, akin to mastering the skill of saying "no," as previously discussed.

Chapter 8
Skills Development Without Getting Overwhelmed

Continued learning without burning out.

It's important to note that finding the right mentors isn't a passive process; it requires effort and dedication. The endeavor to seek out and engage with mentors will certainly be one of the most strategic and fruitful investments you can make. By embracing mentorship, you open doors to accelerated learning, deeper industry insights, and a support network that can propel your career and personal development to new heights.

2) The Power of Microlearning: Microlearning has recently gained traction in professional development. It involves breaking down educational content into bite-sized, digestible chunks. Instead of attending a week-long seminar on a new technique, you could, for instance, watch a 10-minute video or read a short article to get specific instructions on what you need to learn. Hello YouTube!t.

A Journal of Applied Psychology study found that Microlearning makes students 17% more efficient in assimilating information than traditional teaching methods. By absorbing knowledge in small doses, you can seamlessly integrate learning into your daily routine without feeling overwhelmed.

One of the benefits of Microlearning is its feedback loop. Many studies point to significant benefits to applying what you have learned as quickly as possible after taking in the information. Doing so creates a feedback loop that dramatically improves retention of new information.

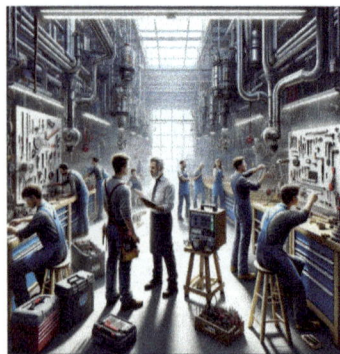

3) Prioritize and Plan: Learning and professional development can often feel overwhelming, especially when you attempt to grasp numerous concepts simultaneously. To effectively manage this, it's crucial to adopt a strategic approach by narrowing your focus to areas most pertinent to your immediate professional needs or future career ambitions. Prioritizing what is essential allows for a more organized and less stressful learning journey.

Setting clear and achievable goals is a key step in this process. For example, if your profession is in the electrical field, and you wish to enhance your expertise, you might specialize in smart home installations. This goal is not only specific but also aligns with emerging trends in the industry, making it a relevant and strategic choice for career advancement.

Skills Development Without Getting Overwhelmed

Continued learning without burning out.

4) Get on a learning schedule: Another vital aspect of effective learning is the creation of a structured schedule. Allocating specific times during the week exclusively for professional development is a powerful strategy. This dedicated block time slot could be used for activities like attending workshops, online courses, or hands-on practice. The importance of this practice lies in its ability to turn learning into a regular habit rather than a perpetual state of 'study mode.'

By doing so, you balance your professional and personal life, reducing the risk of burnout and enhancing the quality of your learning experience.

5) Hands-on Learning: Skilled trades inherently demand a hands-on approach to learning. This necessity stems from recognizing that experiential, or hands-on learning, is significantly more effective than traditional, classroom-based methods for these fields. Research consistently supports this approach, suggesting that engaging directly with the material leads to better comprehension, retention, and practical application of skills.

The National Training Laboratories reveals a stark contrast in retention rates between different learning methods. While the average retention rate for lecture-based learning is only 5%, this rate dramatically increases to 75% when learners are involved in direct, hands-on experience.

An extension to Microlearning, hands-on learning encourages skilled trades professionals to move beyond the passive absorption of information. Instead of just reading about a new technique or concept, it advocates for immersive practice. This could involve participating in interactive workshops, engaging in real-world apprenticeships, or simply experimenting and tinkering in a personal workspace. Such active involvement allows learners to experience the practical application of theories and concepts firsthand, fostering a deeper and more intuitive understanding of their trade.

6) Learning environment is important: As we tackle the subject of work-life balance, your environment, as in the time, place, and state of mind, can dramatically impact interaction and especially retention of the subject matter. For example, try reading an electrical ladder schematic with a baby crying in the background. When you block time out for learning, it's best to plan those times around learning environments that are free of distractions. This can be challenging at times, but it is worth it.

Chapter 8
Skills Development Without Getting Overwhelmed
Balancing job demands with growth opportunities.

Balancing daily job demands and seizing growth opportunities can sometimes feel like a tightrope for those in skilled trades. Thinking about further training or courses might feel overwhelming when you're busy with hands-on tasks.

A 2016 survey from the Pew Research Center showed that 87% of workers believe continuous training and learning are essential in their careers. So, how do we find that sweet spot?

Skilled trades can have periods of intense activity followed by lulls. HVACR technician, for instance, may have weeks packed with back-to-back calls when the weather is excessively hot or cold followed by weeks of moderate weather resulting in mush less work intencity. This cyclical nature is inherent in many trades. Recognizing these patterns allows professionals to time their development activities effectively. Using downtime for upskilling keeps one engaged and ensures you're better prepared for the next rush.

Networking withing your industry: The significance of person-to-person networking must be balanced, particularly in trades and industries where personal connections and reputation are pivotal. The adage "your network is your net worth" resonates profoundly in these sectors, underscoring the immense value of interpersonal relationships in shaping one's career trajectory.

LinkedIn Report: A LinkedIn survey revealed that 85% of job positions are filled through networking channels.

Harvard Report: According to Harvard Business Review, about 80% of job opportunities are not advertised publicly. This finding underscores the hidden job market, where many positions are filled through referrals, internal promotions, or direct contact with candidates.

Both reports highlight the importance of networking and building professional connections, as many of these opportunities are accessible primarily through personal and professional networks rather than traditional job search methods.

By actively networking, professionals stay informed about the latest trends and developments in their respective fields and significantly broaden their access to opportunities that might otherwise remain hidden.

Chapter 8
Skills Development Without Getting Overwhelmed

Leveraging technology for efficient learning.

When we talk about professional development, we often think of endless seminars, workshops, and piles of books. But in the age of technology, improving your skills and knowledge doesn't have to be so overwhelming or traditional. For skilled tradespeople, leveraging technology can make learning more effective, engaging, and adaptable to their needs.

The Rise of Online Platforms and Courses: There's a myth that hands-on trades can't benefit from online learning, but that couldn't be further from the truth. In recent years, MANY online platforms have emerged offering comprehensive courses tailored for specific trades.

According to a report by Inside Higher Ed in 2021, the popularity of online vocational training surged, with enrollment numbers rising by over 20% from the previous year.

These courses employ videos, quizzes, and simulations to ensure learners grasp complex concepts without feeling overwhelmed.

Mobile Apps and the Microlearning Environment: Thanks to smartphones and tablets, skilled tradespeople can now learn on the go, squeezing in a 15-minute lesson during their break or while waiting for a client. In recent years, the popularity of podcasts has brought learning on the go to an entirely new level. Finding experts on specific subjects that matter to the listeners personally or professionally has always been challenging.

Studies, like one from the Journal of Applied Psychology, have found that microlearning using compact technologies like tables and smartphones makes the transfer of learning from the classroom to the desk 17% more efficient.

Interesting fact: A typical field service technician, constantly moving from one job site to another, can spend an average of 3 hours daily stuck in traffic. This time adds up significantly over the course of a year. For a skilled trade worker who is active 350 days per year, the total time spent in traffic can accumulate to approximately 1050 hours. This duration is substantial, equivalent to almost 44 full days each year spent solely in transit.

As discussed earlier in this book, this transit time presents a unique learning opportunity. By safely engaging with trade-related educational content such as podcasts and audiobooks during these periods, technicians can transform what would otherwise be unproductive time into valuable learning experiences.

Chapter 8
Skills Development Without Getting Overwhelmed
Leveraging technology for efficient learning.

Peer Learning Communities: Online communities and peer learning play a crucial role in professional development, offering a treasure trove of collective wisdom and practical advice from an array of industry experts and seasoned professionals.

These virtual platforms, including forums, social media groups, and trade-specific websites, have revolutionized sharing and accessing knowledge.

They empower individuals to engage in dynamic dialogues where they can ask questions, share personal experiences, and offer constructive feedback.

One of the key strengths of these online communities is their ability to break down geographical and institutional barriers, bringing together diverse perspectives from around the globe. This inclusivity enriches the learning experience, exposing professionals to various viewpoints and techniques that might not be available in their immediate environment.

A 2020 survey by the Pew Research Center revealed that over 60% of skilled workers participating in online trade communities reported increased confidence in their professional abilities. The survey also highlights the significant impact peer-to-peer learning and online collaboration can have on an individual's professional growth and confidence.

Massive Open Online Courses (MOOC): These platforms have revolutionized how education is delivered and consumed worldwide. These platforms offer courses across numerous disciplines, enabling learners to acquire new skills, advance their careers, and indulge in lifelong learning from their homes. Beyond the convenience of remote access and a diverse course catalog, one of the key advantages of these platforms is their incorporation of community features. These features facilitate interaction among learners and between learners and instructors or mentors. Here are just a few of such platforms:

Chapter 8
Skills Development Without Getting Overwhelmed

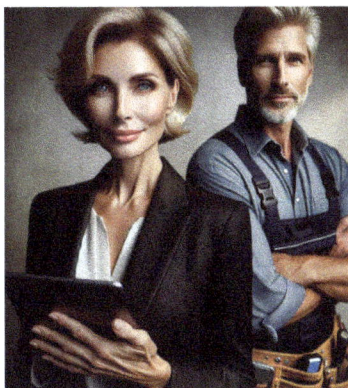

Otto and Carol -Otto, our highly skilled and experienced tradesman, finds himself at a crossroads in his career. The construction industry, his professional home, is undergoing rapid transformation. New technologies and innovative materials are being introduced at an unprecedented pace. Despite his extensive experience, Otto must evolve and master these novel approaches to maintain his relevance and expertise in the field.

During a significant project, Otto faces a critical moment of realization. His traditional techniques, reliable and effective for years, are on the brink of needing to be updated. This awareness propels him to seek advice and wisdom from mentors and colleagues navigating similar challenges.

Recognizing the constraints of his busy schedule, Otto adopts a microlearning strategy. He integrated short, focused block time into his daily routine, concentrating on emerging building methods. This approach lets him stay abreast of industry advancements without overwhelming his packed schedule.

Meanwhile, Carol, a dynamic executive in the high-tech industry, faces her own set of challenges. The tech world is evolving rapidly, and staying at the forefront requires continuous learning and adaptation. Carol's role is demanding, leaving little time for traditional, extensive educational endeavors.

Carol soon discovers an effective learning strategy amidst her busy professional life. She starts weaving educational opportunities into her block time of daily activities, creating an environment of ongoing learning and innovation within her team. Carol ensures collective growth and progress by fostering a culture where new technologies and ideas are regularly shared and explored.

Additionally, Carol turns to online platforms and courses, choosing those offering concise, targeted modules. These learning tools are well-suited to her hectic lifestyle, enabling her to acquire new knowledge and skills in a manageable, efficient manner.

Otto and Carol's stories highlight the necessity of embracing change and finding innovative ways to grow and stay competitive in rapidly evolving professional landscapes.

Chapter 8
Skills Development Without Getting Overwhelmed

Set Clear Learning Goals: Identify the specific skills or knowledge areas you wish to develop. Consider what interests you the most and what will benefit your career as well as personal life. Then, break these larger goals into smaller, achievable steps.

Create a Balanced Schedule: You can allocate specific times each week to focus on learning, making sure these block times don't conflict with your existing work and personal commitments. A well-planned schedule helps maintain a healthy balance, allowing you to progress in your learning without neglecting other important aspects of your life.

Choose Appropriate Learning Resources: Select learning materials that align with your goals, whether online courses, workshops, or books. Look for resources that offer flexibility in pace and time commitment so they can easily fit into your life without causing stress or burnout.

Leverage Technology for Efficiency: Use educational apps and online platforms to enhance your learning experience. These tools can make learning more efficient and help you organize and track your progress, making the process smoother and more engaging.

Apply New Skills at Work: Try to apply the new skills you're learning in your current job. This practical application reinforces your learning and shows your employer your commitment to growth. It can lead to new opportunities and demonstrate your evolving capabilities.

Seek Feedback and Mentorship: Regularly ask supervisors, mentors, or peers for feedback on your progress. This input can provide valuable insights and help you adjust your learning path. Mentorship can also offer guidance, support, and encouragement throughout your learning journey.

Evaluate and Adjust Regularly Periodically review your learning goals and the progress you've made. Be open to adjusting your plan based on changes in job demands, personal interests, or new learning opportunities. Staying flexible allows you to adapt and grow more effectively.

Stay Updated with Technology: Stay informed about new technologies and tools that facilitate learning. Attending webinars, following tech blogs, or joining online communities can help you stay on top of trends and discover new ways to enhance your learning experience.

Chapter 9
Financial Stability and its Role in Balance

In This Chapter

- Economic Advantages of Skilled Trades.

- Loss of Basic Financial Education.

- Budgeting Essentials for Skilled Trades.

- Costs of Overtime in Skilled Trades.

- Savings and Investments for Financial Stability.

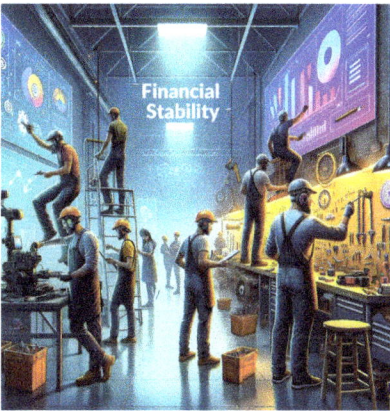

Chapter 9 of the book delves into the crucial topic of financial stability and its significant role in achieving a balanced life, especially for individuals engaged in skilled trades. It begins by exploring the broader economic landscape of the skilled trade sector, shedding light on common misconceptions regarding overtime and its true cost. The chapter emphasizes the importance of financial prudence, guiding readers on how to get their financial affairs in order.

Through a blend of insightful analysis and practical advice, it aims to empower skilled trade workers with the knowledge and tools necessary for achieving and maintaining financial stability, which is portrayed as a foundational pillar for a well-balanced and fulfilling life.

"Do not save what is left after spending, but spend what is left after saving."

- Warren Buffett, CEO of Berkshire Hathaway, has a Net Worth estimated at 127 Billion Dollars

Learn more online about this chapter

Chapter 9
Financial Stability and its Role in Balance
Understanding the skilled trade economy.

BREAKING NEWS

According to the U.S. Bureau of Labor Statistics, as of 2020, many skilled tradespeople earn a median annual wage **higher** than the national average.

Headlines like this suggest that with the right budgeting techniques, individuals in skilled trades can achieve financial stability and even wealth exceeding that of their college-degree counterparts.

However, there's a catch. Many skilled trades professionals operate in a dynamic (ever-changing) demand environment. This means irregular income, unpredictable job durations, and the challenge of covering one's benefits and insurance. Thus, while the earning potential is strong, so is the need for careful financial management.

Financial literacy - How our public schools have failed: In years past, public schools provided basic "Home economics" classes. The classes included instruction on cooking, cleaning, and (ah yes) budgeting.

Specific to the subject of financial literacy, unless their parents happened to be financially literate and took the time to teach their kids this lost art, we now have two generations of Americans with the highest levels of personal debt on record and little to no skills on how to deal with it.

Because of accelerating skilled trade labor shortages, wage levels for most trades, especially for journeymen workers, are accelerating, and that's a good thing. However, the curse of the modern skilled trade pro is that spending tends to accelerate faster than wage growth, largely due to financial illiteracy.

The financial challenges that Gen Y and Gen Z face are due to the MASSIVE failure of America's public education system to prepare our youth for life once they leave home.

As a net result, skilled trades workers have higher-than-average financial challenges despite making great money. When finances get out of control, it's well documented that many unfortunate situations will ensue. These include chronic health issues, marital challenges, and divorce. The worst-case scenarios of work-life imbalance are covered earlier in chapters one and two of this book.

Chapter 9
Financial Stability and its Role in Balance
Understanding the true cost of overtime.

The concept of overtime often holds an appealing shine for those working in skilled trades. The allure of increased pay rates, the potential for a heftier paycheck, and the apparent advantage of maximizing earnings in fewer days are enticing. Who wouldn't want to turn their regular 8-hour shift into a ten or 12-hour endeavor if it means getting more financial security, right? But like any coin, there's another side to this. The implications of consistently working overtime in skilled trades can have hidden costs often overlooked in the excitement of seeing those extra digits on the paycheck.

1) More Income = More Physical and Mental Toll: Let's begin with the most immediate and obvious cost: your health. A study published in the Journal of Occupational and Environmental Medicine (2016) suggested that individuals who consistently worked overtime faced a higher risk of coronary heart disease. Skilled trades often involve manual labor, with workers operating heavy machinery, climbing ladders, or handling electrical equipment. Extended hours can increase fatigue and reduce attention span, and in certain trades, even a moment's distraction can be perilous.

2) Quality of Work and Productivity: According to a research piece by Stanford University, employee output falls sharply after a 50-hour work-week and nosedives after 55 hours to the point where someone working 70 hours produces nothing more with those extra 15. In the skilled trades, where precision and attention to detail are paramount, the quality of work can suffer with prolonged hours. Mistakes due to fatigue or decreased focus can lead to costly reworks or dangerous situations.

3) The Ripple Effect on Personal Life: The "Ripple Effect" is a phenomenon that underscores how an excessively demanding work schedule can have profound implications on various facets of one's personal life. Once vibrant and fulfilling, relationships may suffer due to the lack of quality time and attention required.

Hobbies and personal interests, crucial for individual fulfillment and self-expression, often get sidelined in the relentless pursuit of career goals. The American Sociological Review, in a 2016 article, highlighted this issue, emphasizing that overwork and the resultant scarcity of personal time are among the leading causes of increased stress levels and marital dissatisfaction. This imbalance affects individual well-being and cascades on family life and social relationships, demonstrating the far-reaching consequences of letting work overshadow personal life.

Chapter 9
Financial Stability and its Role in Balance

Understanding the true cost of overtime.

4) Financial Costs of Health Implications: Now, circling back to financial implications, while overtime does promise a fatter paycheck in the short term, the long-term health implications could mean higher medical bills and reduced working days. It's like borrowing time from the future, and the interest rates, in terms of health, can be exorbitant.

5) The Hidden Opportunity Cost: Then there's the opportunity cost. When their primary job completely binds one's time and energy, they miss out on opportunities to upskill, diversify their skills, or even embark on side ventures. In a rapidly evolving job market, continuous learning and flexibility are invaluable. Over-reliance on overtime might result in stagnant skills, which could be a significant disadvantage in the long run.

6) Compromised Physical and Emotional Availability: Even when physically present, the fatigue and stress from overworking can affect a person's emotional and mental availability to their family. They may need more time to engage in meaningful conversations or activities, leading to further disconnection.

Drs. Arnold Bakker and Evangelia Demerouti explain how work-related stress, connected to excessive overtime, can bleed into home life and even impact a partner's well-being. The 'spillover' occurs when work stress is brought home, affecting the individual's focus on social or family life. The 'Crossover' happens when this stress affects the partner, potentially leading to burnout.

Bottom line: For those working in skilled trades, the allure of overtime pay is a significant factor that draws many to willingly extend their working hours. The immediate boost in income that comes with overtime is undeniably appealing, acting as a powerful motivator for those looking to increase their earnings in the short term.

However, it's crucial to step back and consider the broader picture beyond the immediate financial benefits. Engaging in prolonged overtime translates into additional income and more time spent away from family, hobbies, and rest. This shift in work-life balance can lead to various consequences, from physical fatigue and stress to a noticeable strain on personal relationships. Moreover, the opportunity cost of overtime work—such as missed personal development opportunities and the potential for creative pursuits outside of work—can impact long-term satisfaction and well-being. Individuals must weigh these factors carefully, balancing the benefits of extra pay against the potential drawbacks on health, personal growth, and the quality of their relationships.

Chapter 9
Financial Stability and its Role in Balance
Getting your financial house in order

Before applying these tested strategies to put your financial matters in order, it's crucial to understand that everyone's financial situation is unique. Will I see quick results? The answer varies: in some areas, you might notice swift improvements; in others, progress may be slower. The key objective isn't just to start quickly and maintain consistency and dedication over time. With this mindset, you're ready to take the first step. **So, let's get started on this journey together.**

Step#1 - Track Every Dollar: It might sound tedious, but tracking every dollar that comes in and goes out can offer profound insights into spending habits. There are numerous apps and tools designed to simplify this process. Knowing where money is being spent can highlight areas for potential savings or show where additional income can make the most difference. After selecting the app to start tracking where your money is going, try to segment your spending into categories, from the biggest items (such as rent, food, insurance, entertainment, etc.) to the smallest.

Step#2 - Cost reductions: As you start collecting spending data and breaking your spending down into categories, areas you can cut back should become clearer. Entertainment-related subscriptions such as Netflix, Amazon, or Xbox are good examples. If you are like most folks, you are likely being charged for subscription services every month that you rarely or do not use at all.

Data from C+R Research indicates that many consumers (42%) admit they've stopped using a subscription service but forgot they were still paying for it. This is particularly common among younger generations like Gen Z. Almost one-quarter (22%) of consumers feel overwhelmed by the number of subscription services they have, and one-third plan to cut back on subscriptions within the next six months.

To put things in perspective, a subscription that costs $15.00 per month comes to $180.00 per year. If canceling such a subscription only takes 15 minutes, this equates to $720.00 per hour. Good right?

Looking at things this way helps motivate and even justifies the sometimes mind-numbing task of sitting on hold to get something you are not using canceled. And a PRO TIP: always make a note of the customer service representative you spoke to when you change or cancel a subscription. It's also smart to request an email confirming the changes made.

Chapter 9
Financial Stability and its Role in Balance
Getting your financial house in order

Step#3 - The dreaded "B" word: The "B" budget is not all bad. With your newfound ability to track every dollar (step #1) and eliminate the low-hanging fruit expense, it's time for a budget. When you select your every-dollar tracking tool (Step #1), the same tool also provides resources to set budgets for the major categories you set up. If your every-dollar tracking tool does not have a budgeting tool, there are TONS of them. The larger banks often have good tools, PROVIDED that they have resources to export your data, should you want to switch to another budgeting tool.

Step #4 - The Emergency Fund: Given the unpredictability of work, having an emergency fund is vital. A 2019 Bankrate survey indicated that only 40% of Americans could cover a $1,000 emergency from their savings. For skilled trade workers, this number needs to be higher. Ideally, I aim for 3-6 months' worth of expenses. This provides a safety net during lean times or unexpected expenses. Setting aside an emergency fund can go a long way towards building your confidence, especially when changing jobs or when a major expenditure comes up unexpectedly, such as buying a car or replacing a major home appliance.

Step #5 - Debt management short-term and long-term: Navigating the journey from debt to financial stability requires a strategic blend of short-term management and long-term planning, especially regarding consumer debt. Initially, it's crucial to tackle high-interest debts head-on. This often means prioritizing credit card balances, personal loans, and other high-rate obligations. Establishing a solid budget and cutting unnecessary expenses **(Steps 1 &2)** can free up additional funds to tackle debt. Although seemingly counterintuitive when facing debt, an emergency savings fund **(Step 4)** is essential to prevent falling deeper into debt during unexpected financial setbacks.

In the realm of long-term strategy, consider the snowball or avalanche methods. The snowball method involves paying off debts from smallest to largest, building momentum as each balance is cleared. Conversely, the avalanche method first targets debts with the highest interest rates, potentially saving more money over time. Both strategies encourage discipline and consistency, key components in the debt reduction journey.

Expanding upon these strategies, incorporating tools like debt consolidation loans or balance transfer credit cards can also effectively manage high-interest debts more efficiently. These methods can lower interest rates and consolidate payments, making debt management more manageable. SEE QR link at the end this .. >

Financial Stability and its Role in Balance

Getting your financial house in order

..> to access the latest tips on managing your debt and avoiding getting ripped off.

Additionally, seeking professional financial advice or counseling can provide personalized strategies tailored to individual circumstances, ensuring a more directed and effective approach to debt management.

Long-term financial health also involves reevaluating spending habits and potentially increasing income through side hustles or career advancement. Education on financial literacy is paramount.

Moreover, embracing a mindset shift towards money and debt is vital. Understanding and addressing the psychological triggers that lead to overspending can prevent future debt. Engaging with communities supporting financial independence and learning from others' experiences can inspire and motivate individuals on their journey to debt freedom.

Remember, while everyone's path to debt-freeness is unique, discipline, strategic planning, continuous learning, and a supportive community are universal pillars of success. According to a National Foundation for Credit Counseling survey, a proactive approach to managing debt improves financial outcomes and enhances overall well-being.

Step #6 - Long-term investing: With Steps 1 through 4 out of the way, it's time for long-term investing. Although my role is never to give investment advice, here is some helpful general information to get you started. Once you've built up your emergency fund, it's time to consider investing. Compound interest, often called the 8th wonder of the world by finance aficionados, works best over longer periods. Starting early is key.

For skilled tradespeople, this could mean investing in trade-specific tools or equipment for more significant job opportunities or venturing into side businesses. Moreover, there's the stock market. Let's take a simple example. If you start investing just $200 a month from age 25, assuming a 7% annual return, by the time you're 65, you could have amassed over $500,000, even if the total you invested out of pocket was just $96,000. The earlier and more consistently you invest, the more you stand to gain.

Retirement and Skilled Trades: Retirement might seem like a distant reality when you're in the prime of your working life, but it sneaks up faster than you'd think. According to the Economic Policy Institute, the mean retirement savings of all working-age families in the US is only about $95,776.

Chapter 9
Financial Stability and its Role in Balance
Getting your financial house in order

More is needed for a comfortable retirement, especially with increasing life expectancies. For skilled tradespeople, regularly contributing to a retirement account like a 401(k) or Roth IRA can make all the difference in ensuring a relaxed, financially secure retirement.

Financial stability isn't about earning a sky-high salary. It's about wise decisions, consistent savings, and smart investments. Skilled trades offer a robust platform to build this stability, and with the right choices, anyone in this field can achieve the balance and flexibility they desire in their financial life.

This interesting graphic illustrates the magic of compounding interest over time. Making regular contributions to your long-term investment plan can yield some amazing results. The sooner you start, the better.

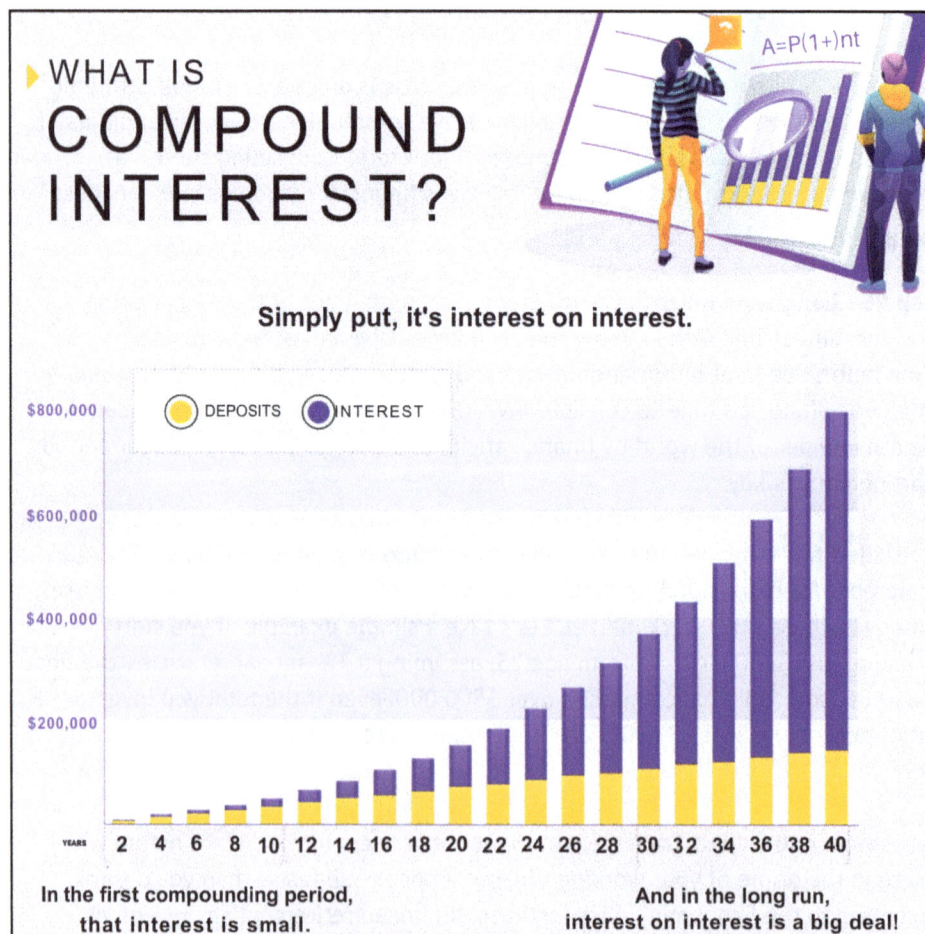

▸ WHAT IS
COMPOUND INTEREST?

$A = P(1+)nt$

Simply put, it's interest on interest.

● DEPOSITS ● INTEREST

YEARS: 2 4 6 8 10 12 14 16 18 20 22 24 26 28 30 32 34 36 38 40

In the first compounding period, that interest is small.

And in the long run, interest on interest is a big deal!

Chapter 9
Financial Stability and its Role in Balance

Otto and Carol - Their story took a turn when Otto faced a harsh winter season. The couple confronted the reality of their unpreparedness for such lean times. It was a wake-up call to practice what they preached about financial wisdom. The couple sat down with bank statements, bills, and a determination to chart a new course.

They embraced the "dreaded B-word" – budgeting. Carol introduced Otto to digital tools for tracking expenses while Otto meticulously logged every transaction. Together, they identified unnecessary expenses and created a plan to build an emergency fund with the money they saved, canceling subscriptions they no longer needed, changing their cell phone plans, and even selling some things around the house they no longer needed.

The couple's efforts bore fruit sooner than expected. When a major client delayed payment, Otto was not plunged into the financial chaos that would have ensued a year ago. Their emergency fund provided the buffer they needed.

How Americans would cover an emergency $1,000 bill

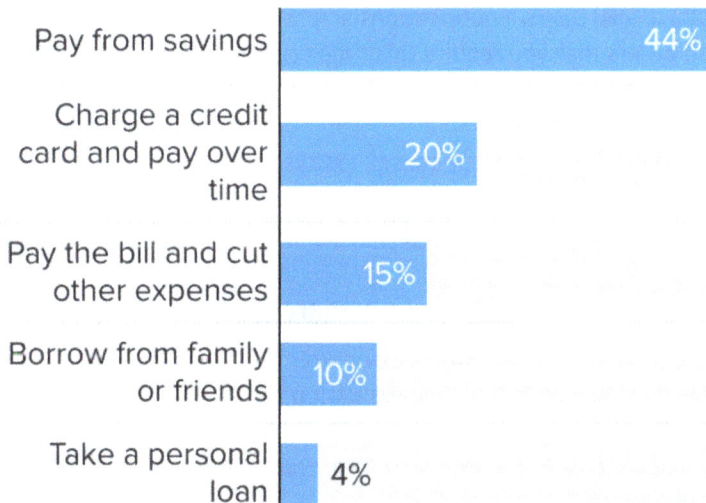

- Pay from savings: 44%
- Charge a credit card and pay over time: 20%
- Pay the bill and cut other expenses: 15%
- Borrow from family or friends: 10%
- Take a personal loan: 4%

Note: A telephone survey of 1,004 American adults conducted in January

Source: Bankrate

Chapter 9 - Checkup

In previous chapters, assessments were made regarding your overall work-life equilibrium, signs of imbalance between work and life, and managing time. This fourth and final assessment focuses on personal finances. The selection of these subjects was intentional, chosen from the book's content because they represent the most frequent reasons for work-life balance difficulties within the skilled trades sector.

Instructions

As we approach this pivotal moment in our exploration of managing personal finances within the skilled trades sector, let's ensure we're fully prepared for this evaluation. Adhering to these guidelines will optimize your benefits from this introspective exercise.

Organize Your Environment

Seek a Solitary Spot: Select a place where interruptions are minimal. This could be a quiet room or a calm outdoor area, aiming for a setting that fosters concentrated thought.

Remove Distractions: Disable notifications across your devices to prevent breaks in focus. Inform others that you require this time undistracted, emphasizing the importance of minimizing distractions for your self-reflection.

Prioritize Comfort: Make sure your chosen area is well-lit and has comfortable seating. I want you to know that ensuring your environment is good enough to support sustained attention and mitigate any physical distractions during your review.

Timing Considerations

Select an Optimal Moment: Plan your evaluation for when you feel most alert and at ease, typically in the morning within the initial hours after awakening. Avoid scheduling it close to or right after work to prevent the impact of tiredness or stress on your insights.

Ready Your Mind and Body: Partake in mild exercise or meditation beforehand. These practices can clear your head, lessen stress, and create a constructive self-evaluation tone.

Chapter 9 - Checkup

Instructions
- Responding to Questions Continued -

Answering the Questions

Value Honesty: View this evaluation as a chance for genuine introspection. There are correct responses, merely truthful reflections on your financial management status. Your candor is very important for a true self-assessment.

Follow Your First Impression: Please trust your immediate reaction to each query. Your first instinct often mirrors your actual situation and feelings, so avoid overanalyzing your responses.

Move Past Sticking Points: If you are hesitating on a question, you can see it as a cue to proceed. Dwelling too long on a single query can disrupt the assessment flow and might not lead to more precise conclusions.

Pause to Center

It's a good idea to center yourself before beginning the checkup, and it's a preliminary action. It ensures you enter this self-examination with the necessary clarity and peace. Taking a break from the day's hustle to create a reflective mental space is crucial for delving deeply into your financial management practices. This initial step is the foundation for a more engaged and insightful assessment.

Finally, I'd like you to approach this evaluation with openness and a desire for growth, allowing it to spark positive transformations. This journey toward mastering personal finance management, specially tailored for the skilled trades, is a step toward a life that embodies your highest goals and principles. Embrace this opportunity with zeal and readiness for the personal development that awaits. There are absolutely no wrong answers. If your results suggest areas for enhancement, I will make recommendations before I move to the next chapter.

Chapter 9 - Checkup

Step 1: Read each scenario in the left column. Then, circle a 1, 2, or 3 if.............

1 = RARELY happens | 2 = Happens ONCE IN A WHILE | 3 = Happens ALL THE TIME.

Step 2: Once you have scored each item, write your "Your total Score: >" at the bottom of the page in the box provided.

1) How often do you find yourself unable to stick to your budget due to unexpected expenses?		1 2 3
2) To what extent do you feel that personal debts impact your daily peace of mind?		1 2 3
3) How frequently do you postpone or neglect savings for future goals or emergencies?		1 2 3
4) Challenges with personal finances comes up in conversations with your significant other.		1 2 3
5) How often do you encounter stress due to balancing work income with personal spending?		1 2 3
6) To what degree do you feel unprepared for financial emergencies or downturns work opportunities?		1 2 3
7) How frequently do you plan to reassess your financial goals and strategies for improvement but never get to it?		1 2 3
8) How much do you struggle with separating personal things you actually need from things that you want?		1 2 3
9) To what extent does financial planning take a backseat due to workload or day to day life?		1 2 3
10) How often do you find yourself lacking resources for personal development or leisure due to financial constraints?		1 2 3
11) To what degree do you feel your current financial management practices hinder your work-life balance?		1 2 3
12) How frequently do you experience difficulty in investing in tools, equipment, or professional development due to financial limitations?		1 2 3
Your Total Score ---	>>	

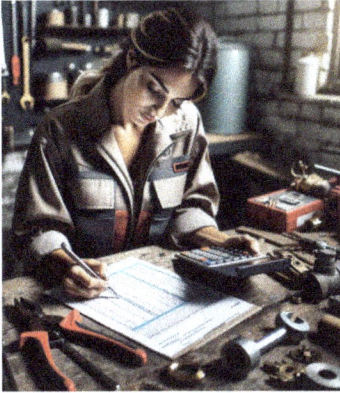

If your score falls within the "Optimal" category, it indicates your proficiency in managing personal finances within the skilled trades sector, showing a balanced approach with minimal financial stress. For those with scores in the "Moderate" or "Challenged" ranges, reflect on the suggested methods to improve your financial health, focusing on better financial management of your trade and personal expenses.

Optimal Financial Management (Score 12-20): This score reflects superior management of trade-related and personal finances, with individuals adeptly separating their business expenses from personal spending. They maintain financial stability, ensuring savings for personal enjoyment and future investments. These individuals excel in keeping their financial commitments well-organized, enabling them to enjoy leisure without financial worries encroaching on their time off. I suggest continuing vigilance to maintain this financial health. If you achieved an optimal score, congratulations. Please review the subsequent page's recommendations, which might still offer value.

Moderate Financial Management (Score 21-29): Those within this score range occasionally need help maintaining a distinct separation between their trade-related financial obligations and personal expenditures. Financial planning might only sometimes persist, leading to sporadic concerns over financial security. There may be moments when financial considerations intrude upon personal time, hindering the ability to allocate resources towards personal goals and self-improvement. It's recommended for individuals in this category to regularly evaluate their financial management techniques and consider strategies to prevent financial matters from overly affecting their personal lives.

Challenged Financial Management (Score 30-36): Individuals scoring here encounter significant difficulties in effectively managing their finances between their trade and personal lives, often experiencing financial strain. This strain can lead to increased stress, the risk of financial instability, and the neglect of savings for personal and family needs. Those with high scores should urgently reevaluate their financial strategies, seeking advice and implementing steps to prioritize financial health and achieve a more stable balance between trade obligations and personal financial goals.

Chapter 9 - Checkup Recommendations

Based on this evaluation, the insights provided are invaluable for those in skilled trades working to enhance their personal finance management. Suppose your score indicates more frequent financial management challenges. In that case, it highlights the importance of adopting measures to refine your financial strategies, alleviate financial stress, and achieve a more balanced financial life. Here are several recommendations aimed at improving your financial health.

Challenged Financial Management (Score 30-36)

Adopting Simple Financial Planning Tools: Instead of complex software, consider simple, user-friendly budgeting apps or spreadsheets that effectively track income and expenses.

Scheduled Financial Check-ins: Regularly set aside time each week for a financial review session to assess budget adherence and adjust plans as needed, making it a habit for financial control.

Essential Spending Analysis: Evaluate your spending habits to identify and eliminate non-essential expenses, increasing savings and financial security.

Goal-Oriented Saving Plans: Create specific saving goals for short-, medium-, and long-term financial objectives, using automated savings plans to ensure consistency.

Integrating Financial Education into Daily Routine: Incorporate financial literacy into your daily life through short articles, videos, or podcasts that can be consumed in your downtime.

Peer Review of Financial Practices: Share financial strategies with peers for constructive feedback, gaining insights into effective financial management habits and potential areas for improvement.

Exploring Alternative Financial Resources: Look beyond traditional financial advice, exploring blogs, forums, and online communities focused on financial independence and money management techniques.

Also, consider the advice for scores in the 21-29 range for further enhancements.

Moderate Financial Management (Score Range: 21-29)

Selective Financial Information Consumption: Choose a limited number of reliable financial news sources to stay informed without becoming overwhelmed by the volume of information.

Learning through Financial Workshops: Attend workshops or webinars that offer practical advice on budgeting, investing, and saving, tailored to those in the skilled trades.

Automated Expense Tracking: Utilize apps that automatically categorize expenses and highlight areas where spending can be reduced, simplifying budget management.

Open Financial Planning Sessions: Engage in monthly financial planning discussions with family or financial advisors to align on goals, budgets, and strategies.

Leveraging Downtime for Financial Growth: Dedicate leisure periods to learning new financial skills or exploring investment opportunities that can contribute to long-term wealth.

Daily Financial Goal Alignment: Start each day by reviewing financial priorities and adjusting daily spending decisions to better align with your overall financial goals.

Efficiency in Financial Task Management: Implement time-saving techniques like batch processing for bill payments and financial planning to reduce the time spent on routine financial tasks.

These recommendations aim to provide varied approaches to achieving financial stability and growth tailored to skilled trades professionals' unique challenges in managing their finances.

For more information and tools to help you improve your time management skills, stop by our site by scanning the QR below.

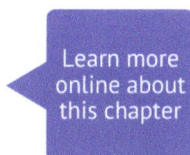

Learn more online about this chapter

Chapter 10
The employee/employer relationship

In This Chapter

- Exploring Work-Life Balance in Skilled Trades.

- Open Dialogue with Employers,

- Offering Solutions, Not Just Problems.

- Using Data to Support Your Case.

- Advocacy for Change in Skilled Trades:

Chapter 10 delves into the intricacies of the employee-employer relationship within the context of achieving a balanced life. It underscores the importance of communicating with employers about the need for balance, advocating for roles or positions that align with personal needs and values, and actively seeking changes in the workplace to foster a healthier work environment. This chapter is pivotal for skilled trade workers looking to navigate the complexities of their careers while maintaining personal well-being and advocating for systemic changes that support work-life harmony.

"Management is doing things right; leadership is doing the right things."

– Peter Drucker, an Austrian-born American management consultant, educator, and author, whose writings contributed significantly to the philosophical and practical foundations of the modern business corporation.

Learn more online about this chapter

Chapter 10
The employee/employer relationship

Communicating with employers about balance.

In Chapter #3, we looked at "The power of NO in professional settings." In that chapter, we explored how to say no gracefully. In this chapter, we will add some higher-level concepts that should be helpful in your quest to have a productive dialog with your boss about work-life balance and potentially be seen as a leader, provided you go about it correctly.

During these times of increasing skilled trade labor shortages, most employers are sensitive to burnout and how an unscheduled absence, commonly related to worker burnout, can impact the business's bottom line. They are also generally aware that burnout can dramatically increase the potential for on-the-job injuries that can result in increased operating costs, such as increased insurance premiums, long after a worker gets back to work.

For conscientious workers who see work-life balance challenges popping up for themselves and coworkers, it's always smart to raise these issues with company management. When you see areas for improvement (avoiding the word " problems "), you can take notes on what you see <u>and</u> ideas for solutions. Once you have these, here are some steps to approach your boss without leaving the impression that your "That Person" is just a complainer, etc.

Timing is important: Ask your boss for a meeting before or after work hours whenever possible. Be ready to answer the <u>"what's this about the question"</u> if it arises. Should this question be asked, save the next five minutes explaining yourself. Just share a general statement like, <u>"I discovered some areas that may help improve work-life balance in the company, and I would like to know what you think."</u>

Open Dialogue is Key: When meeting time comes, you can approach your boss with an open mind. Remember, it's not about demanding change but opening a dialogue. Most employers value feedback, especially when it can lead to a happier, more productive, and safer workforce.

Providing Solutions, Not Just Problems: As we discussed, when you get an opportunity to present areas of improvement to your boss, have a solution, ideally more than one, to present. In doing so, you can avoid the stigma of being a complainer. If your ideas are good, it will be good for your career.

I'd like to follow up with you: Depending on your company's size and management structure, be prepared to have your solutions bounced around within the organization. Before you begin your first meeting with your boss, please ask them if a follow-up meeting is needed.

Chapter 10
The employee/employer relationship

Seeking roles or positions that align with personal needs.

Let's begin by understanding what we mean by 'personal needs.' This can encompass anything from preferred working hours, physical requirements, work-life balance, and proximity to home to even the team dynamics in which you thrive.

A study by the Harvard Business Review showed that employees whose personal values aligned with their job roles and workplace were more engaged, satisfied, and likely to stick around longer.

Why Alignment Matters: Looking at some numbers, according to the Bureau of Labor Statistics, the turnover rate in the skilled trades is higher than the average across all industries. One reason? A mismatch between job demands and personal needs. Remember, a misaligned job isn't just about discomfort. It could mean more sick days, injuries, burnout, and, yes, daydreaming about quitting and running a surf shack in Bali.

Making the Right Choices: For those fresh out of trade school or apprenticeships, it's tempting to jump into the first job offer that comes your way. But hold on a minute! A moment of reflection is in order here. Think about your needs. Do you have a family and prefer reporting to one site each day? Or maybe you love varied challenges and would relish being on a roving team, traveling from one project to another. Whatever it is, always try to filter your employment selections through your family and personal needs.

Having Those Conversations: Once you've pinpointed the position and/or company that you want, it's time to have open conversations with potential employers. The skilled trades, like many industries, are evolving. Many employers are recognizing the need for flexibility and the importance of ensuring their workers are in roles that fit them like a snug glove. So, speak up! Discuss your shift preferences and growth potential, and by all means, take the time to understand as much as possible about THE expectations of the job.

HELPFUL TIPS When first starting in the trade, you may be presented with a written job description. This can be several pages of detailed information or a more simple yet very vague bullet point list.

When presented with such documents, it's best to ensure you fully understand what's expected. Several times in this book, I have been suggested to get a mentor. Having a mentor who has been around the block can give you the between-the-line context of what your employers expect of you, and this can be VERY valuable information.

Chapter 10
The employee/employer relationship
Advocating skilled trades skill advancement.

The drive towards personal and professional growth is not just beneficial; it's essential. As workers navigate the complexities of modern industry, the pursuit of skill advancement emerges as a pivotal force in shaping the trajectory of individual careers and the collective efficacy of teams and organizations. This idea underscores the importance of advocating for continuous learning and development within the trades, offering a roadmap for individuals eager to champion this cause.

Through the strategic sharing of knowledge and the fostering of informal learning environments, skilled trade workers can ignite a culture of perpetual improvement, creating ripples that extend far beyond the confines of their immediate workspaces. This process involves not just the transmission of technical skills and know-how but also the sharing of insights, experiences, and innovative practices that challenge the status quo and inspire excellence. These experiences provide a safe space for asking questions, making mistakes, and experimenting with new methods, essential for innovation.

Here are a few things any skilled trade workers can try in their work environment to advocate for skill development that inherently leads to better work-life balance and overall quality of life:

1. Share Articles or Videos: Bookmark interesting articles or videos that discuss new technologies or techniques in your field. Share these during breaks or via email, noting why you found them interesting or how they might be useful for your work. This casual approach can spark interest and conversations about skill development without any formal setting.

2. Suggest Practical Training Sessions: Could you propose a short, informal session where team members can gather during lunch or after hours to learn something new? You could start with a topic that is relevant to your team. This creates a relaxed environment for learning and sharing knowledge, making it more approachable and less like mandatory training.

3. Be a Positive Example: Take an online course or attend a workshop, then apply what you've learned to your work. Share your experience and results with your colleagues, highlighting practical benefits. Demonstrating personal and professional growth from skill development can motivate others to pursue their learning.

The employee/employer relationship
Advocating for change in the workplace.

4. Use Team Meetings: When discussing work progress or challenges during team meetings, bring up a skill or knowledge area that could improve efficiency or outcomes. Could you suggest a group effort to learn more about it? Integrating skill development into regular work discussions makes it part of the ongoing conversation about improving work quality and team performance.

5. Offer to Help Others: If you notice a colleague struggling with a task that you're skilled in, offer to show them how to do it more effectively. This can be done in a supportive, friendly manner. Peer-to-peer learning strengthens team bonds and encourages a culture where people feel comfortable seeking help and learning from each other.

6. Highlight Safety and Efficiency: When you learn a new technique or tool that makes work safer or more efficient, share this with your team and supervisor, focusing on the tangible benefits. Emphasizing the practical advantages of skill development, especially regarding safety and time-saving, can make a compelling case for its importance.

7. Request Feedback: After you complete a task or project, please ask your supervisor for feedback. Use this as an opportunity to discuss ways to improve further, including any specific training or skills you believe could help. You're committed to continuous improvement and constructively open a dialogue about professional development.

8. Be Solution-Oriented: Identify specific challenges your team faces and research training or learning resources that address these issues. Present these solutions to your team or supervisor to overcome the challenges. By linking skill development directly to solving work-related problems, you're providing clear, actionable reasons why investing in learning is beneficial.

9. Encourage Mentorship Programs: If you are in a team leadership position, pair more experienced team members with those newer to the field or organization in a mentor-mentee relationship.

Encourage regular catch-up sessions where they can discuss career paths, specific skills development, and any work-related challenges. Mentorship provides personalized guidance and support, making skill development and career progression more accessible and less intimidating for newer employees. For mentors, it's an opportunity to refine their leadership and coaching skills. This program strengthens interpersonal relationships within the team and promotes a culture where knowledge and experience are valued and shared willingly.

The employee/employer relationship

Be Direct but Polite: Politely decline additional commitments when necessary, using a response like, "Thank you for thinking of me, but I can't commit to this right now."

Offer an Alternative: If unable to take on a project, suggest someone else who might be interested or available. Consider offering to check in or mentor the person if needed. This approach can benefit everyone involved.

Express Gratitude: Show appreciation for opportunities to maintain positive relationships even when declining them. A response like, "I appreciate the offer, but I'm currently swamped with other projects, can be effective.

Understand Role and Expectations: Gain clarity on job roles and expectations to avoid over-commitment and unnecessary overtime. Ask questions and seek a clear understanding of what's expected.

Acknowledge the Real Cost of Overtime: Working excessive hours can lead to diminished returns, burnout, and health issues. Recognize when extra hours are doing more harm than good.

Work Smart, Not Just Hard: Utilize tools and technologies to improve efficiency. Focus on tasks that yield maximum results and delegate or drop less substantial tasks.

Set Specific Times for Personal Activities: Schedule time for family activities and personal relaxation, like phone-free hours or specific times for walks or meals.

Reevaluate Boundaries Regularly: As life circumstances change, reassess personal and professional boundaries to ensure they remain relevant and effective.

"Every problem has a solution. You just have to be creative enough to find it."

– Travis Kalanick co-founded Uber, a ride-sharing company that revolutionized transportation services globally.

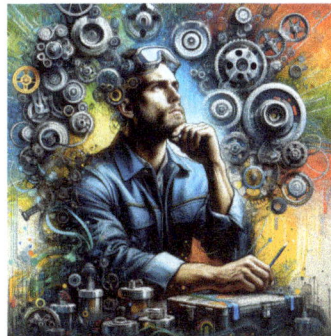

Conclusion

This book has traversed the realms of skill advancement, financial stability, and the delicate art of balancing work demands with the joys and necessities of personal life. As we conclude, it's essential to reflect on the core principles that guide skilled tradespeople through their careers and enrich their lives beyond what they do to make a good living.

Embracing and leveraging it as a tool for growth. Our protagonists, Otto and Carol, share stories that highlight the importance of adaptability and continuous learning. Their experiences underscore that staying relevant in rapidly changing industries requires an unwavering faith and commitment to self-improvement and the willingness to explore new technologies, methodologies, and learning paths.

Financial stability emerges as a foundational pillar, enabling skilled tradespeople to navigate the uncertainties of their professions confidently. Drawing from the wisdom of financial experts and seasoned tradespeople, this book's advice emphasizes the critical role of budgeting, saving, investing, and managing debt. These practices safeguard financial health and support a balanced and fulfilling life.

Another focal point is the relationship between employers and employees in skilled trades. Open dialogue, mutual respect, and the pursuit of arrangements that accommodate individual needs while meeting organizational goals create an environment for a balanced life.

As we wrap up our time together, let us remember that the path of skilled trades is as much about building structures and creating tangible outcomes as it is about building character and shaping lives. The journey is marked by continuous learning, resilience in the face of challenges, and the joy of achievement. To all skilled tradespeople, keep your tools ready, your minds open, and your spirits high. Embrace each day as an opportunity to learn, grow, and make a difference in your world.

Ultimately, the balance we seek is between work and life and within ourselves—between our ambitions and well-being, our efforts and contributions to the community, our pursuit of success, and our commitment to values. This book is a guide, a companion, and a reflection of that quest for balance, offering insights and strategies to navigate the complexities of modern trades and life.

Here's to the skilled tradespeople—may your journey be filled with growth, balance, and fulfillment. **The journey continues, and it is yours to shape.**

Setting Personal and Professional Boundaries Title / Author / Description	QR to Book on Amazon
"Boundaries: When to Say Yes, How to Say No to Take Control of Your Life" by Henry Cloud and John Townsend – A comprehensive guide on establishing healthy boundaries in both personal and professional life.	
"Set Boundaries, Find Peace: A Guide to Reclaiming Yourself" by Nedra Glover Tawwab – Offers practical advice on setting boundaries to improve mental health and personal relationships.	
"Where to Draw the Line: How to Set Healthy Boundaries Every Day" by Anne Katherine – This book delves into the nuances of setting and maintaining healthy boundaries in various aspects of life, including work and personal relationships.	

Time Management for the Tradesperson Title / Author / Description	QR to Book on Amazon
"The 7 Habits of Highly Effective People: Powerful Lessons in Personal Change" by Stephen R. Covey – While not exclusively about time management, this book offers essential effective principles, including prioritizing and planning, that directly apply to time management.	
"Atomic Habits" by James Clear is an Easy and Proven Way to Build Good Habits and Break Bad Ones.	
"Getting Things Done: The Art of Stress-Free Productivity" by David Allen – Introduces a work-life management system that helps with time management and productivity.	

Recourses
Recommended Books

Role of Faith in Maintaining Balance in Your Life Title / Author / Description	QR to Book on Amazon
The Case for Christ: A Journalist's Personal Investigation of the Evidence for Jesus by Lee Stroble. Former atheist and Chicago Tribune journalist Lee Strobel takes an investigative look at the evidence from the fields of science, philosophy, and history.	
"Walking with God: Talk to Him. Hear from Him. Really." by John Eldredge – This book explores the importance of a personal relationship with God as a foundation for finding balance and direction in life.	

Financial Stability and its Role in Balance Title / Author / Description	QR to Book on Amazon
"The Total Money Makeover: A Proven Plan for Financial Fitness" by Dave Ramsey – Provides a straightforward approach to debt reduction, budgeting, and financial planning for stability.	
"Rich Dad Poor Dad" by Robert T. Kiyosaki – Offers lessons on financial literacy, investing, and the importance of understanding money for achieving financial independence.	
"I Will Teach You to Be Rich" by Ramit Sethi – Focuses on creating a no-nonsense approach to personal finance and investing that can lead to financial independence and stability.	
"Personal Finance Made Easy for Young Adults by Dakota A. McQueen. Discover How to Pay Off Debt Faster, Raise Your Credit Score, and Achieve Financial Freedom by Budgeting and Creating Multiple Income Streams"	

Please be aware: Legacy Companies LLC (DBA) SkilledTradeRescue.com receives a small commission when you buy books or other items through the QR link found in this book. Rest assured, the prices of these products remain identical to those offered directly on Amazon. We sincerely appreciate your support.

Recommended Books

The Employee/Employer Relationship Title / Author / Description	QR to Book on Amazon
"The Five Dysfunctions of a Team: A Leadership Fable" by Patrick Lencioni – Offers insights into the dynamics of how teams work and the role of leadership in fostering a positive and productive employee/employer relationship.	
"Crucial Conversations: Tools for Talking When Stakes Are High" by Kerry Patterson, Joseph Grenny, Ron McMillan, and Al Switzler – Provides strategies for effective communication in high-stakes workplace situations, improving relationships between employees and employers.	
"Drive: The Surprising Truth About What Motivates Us" by Daniel H. Pink – Examines the importance of motivation in the workplace and its impact on the employee/employer relationship.	

Time Management Apps

Google Calendar: Perfect for scheduling and receiving reminders for important dates and appointments. This app is also integrated with most smartphones.

Trello: For organizing tasks using boards, lists, and cards. It is great for both personal and team use.

Todoist: A task management tool that helps create and manage to-do lists effectively.

Asana: Excellent for team projects, allowing users to assign tasks to others and set deadlines.

Microsoft To Do: Integrates with Office 365 and helps manage daily tasks.

RescueTime: Tracks time spent on applications and websites, giving insights into productivity.

Evernote: A note-taking app that helps keep all your ideas and tasks in one place.

TimeTree: Useful for sharing and coordinating schedules with family, friends, or colleagues.

Thank You

Martin P. King
SkilledTradeRescue.com

I appreciate your willingness to accompany me on this literary adventure. It is not just appreciated; it is deeply cherished. The journey these pages embark upon is one of discovery, not only for the characters within but also for myself as the creator and, I hope, for you as the reader.

Every individual who turns these pages brings their background, experiences, and emotions to the story, transforming it into something new and extraordinary with each read. Your engagement with this narrative breathes life into it, making each reader's journey through its chapters invaluable to the book's ongoing story. As such, your thoughts, reflections, and critiques are not just welcome but essential. They contribute to a larger dialogue about the work, influencing my growth as a writer and assisting potential readers in deciding whether to embark on this journey themselves.

In light of this, please take a moment to scan the QR code below. This simple act of sharing your review on Amazon can have a profound impact. Your feedback is not merely a critique or praise but a beacon for others navigating the vast seas of literature, seeking their next great adventure. It also serves as a guiding light, offering insights and perspectives crucial for my development as a storyteller. Once again, I extend my heartfelt thanks for your time, engagement, and voice. The path of storytelling is one of connection and shared experiences, and readers like you make this journey not only possible but incredibly fulfilling. Your support is the cornerstone of this adventure; I am eternally grateful for that.

Please consider leaving your reviews on my work on Amazon and THANK YOU again.

www.ingramcontent.com/pod-product-compliance
Lightning Source LLC
Chambersburg PA
CBHW070046100426
42740CB00013B/2816